RELIGION THE TROJAN HORSE OF CHRISTIANITY

BY

EMIL MULLINS

Copyright

Dedication

I dedicate this book first and foremost to the one who truly wrote it. My heavenly Father has been with me every step of the way, and His love and faithfulness are beyond the ability of words to express. Thank you for the privilege and honor of walking with you.

The second person I want to dedicate this book to is my wonderful wife, Mary, who, next to the Lord, is closest to me. Thank you so much for sticking with me through the hard times. I love you. In hindsight, I can now see and understand God's wisdom in selecting just the right helpmate for the work He has called us to. This knowledge has given both of us a foundation for our marriage that has held us together through some difficult times. With God's love and direction, the difficult times became the catalyst for growth and maturity. The struggle toward a holy life and a dedicated life before the Lord has been one we have made together, and for her presence at my side, I will be eternally grateful.

Third, my brother Gary has worked with me in giving valuable input. I so appreciate his help and the Lord's direction in our being able to work together.

Fourth, I would like to dedicate this book to all those who have worked with the Lord in teaching and training me throughout the years. God has richly blessed me with some wonderful brothers and sisters who have all invested in me and are certainly apart of this book. I will not name names as I could not possibly remember all and would not want to leave anyone out. Thank you for your love, patience, and faithfulness.

Table of Contents

Introduction

I have considered writing this book for years and am finally undertaking to do so. My goal is to expose some major strategies of the enemy in the warfare between the kingdom of darkness and the kingdom of light and to unmask some of the cunning lies of the enemy. Satan's lies have kept millions from salvation, as well as the victorious lives of many Christians. Nothing is sacred or true to Lucifer. He lies about God, the gospel, sin, the new birth, and, as a matter of fact, he lies about everything. In truth, he is not only a liar but he is the father of all lies. The following scripture from the book of John are the words of Jesus to the Jews.

John 8:44 You are of your father the devil, and the lusts of your father you will do. He was a murderer from the beginning, and did not abide in the truth because there is no truth in him. When he speaks a lie, he speaks of his own, for he is a liar and the father of it.

The enemy's mission is plainly identified from the Bible, and it is also distinctly contrasted with the mission of Jesus. The following verse identifies his agenda. This verse also declares the desire of God for everyone, namely life and life to the fullest.

John 10:10 The thief does not come except to steal and to kill and to destroy. I have come so that they might have life, and that they might have *it* more abundantly.

In the Greek, the word abundantly means exceeding abundantly, beyond what is expected, imagined, or hoped for. This is the life the Lord wants for all His children. What an amazing contrast to the devil's mission to steal, kill, and destroy. Jesus and the evil one are diametrically opposed.

Deception is one of the main ways the devil can affect the lives of so many people. He is the master of lies and is, by nature, a deceiver. If he can get you to believe a lie, then your life will be affected by that lie; in fact, you may even find yourself living the lie. There is an amazing promise in the scriptures:

John 8:31 Then Jesus said to the Jews who believed on Him, "If you continue in My Word, you are My disciples indeed. **32** And you shall know the truth, and the truth shall make you free."

Verse 32 is often misunderstood and misquoted. The inaccurate quote is, "the truth will set you free." That is not what the scripture says. It says if you hold to my teaching, you are really my disciples, then you will know the truth, and the truth will set you free. Freedom does not just come from knowing the truth, it comes from knowing Jesus, as Jesus is the truth. So many people who are members of the Christian religion do not know Him. I won't name the religion, but I have spoken to many who, although they have been faithful in church attendance and giving, etc., had never even heard of Jesus. This was baffling to me.

However, It is true in so many religions. They are faithful to their religion but have never met the savior. Jesus is the truth. Even knowing the truth about Jesus does not mean that you actually know Jesus. Christianity is not just a religion it is a relationship with God the Father, Jesus the Son, and the Holy Spirit. Jesus declares to us this truth in the following scripture.

John 14:6 Jesus said to him, "I am the Way, the Truth, and the Life; no one comes to the Father but by Me."

This book is not a deep theological dissertation. Its purpose is to make it as plain and understandable as possible that the lie of salvation through religion is the most cunning and deceptive tool the enemy has ever devised. It has literally led millions of people to a life void of a relationship with Jesus, who is the only means of salvation. Religious duties and good works are not bad in themselves, but they are void of any means of earning or obtaining salvation. I am not talking about bad people. God forbid that my efforts in this book would ever come across as judgmental or critical. It is not about an attack on anyone but a desire to speak the truth concerning some very important areas. It may be a good tool for discipleship, and it also can help those of us who have been Christians for years and yet have not understood some of the basic things that can make all the difference in our lives.

NOTE: All scripture references are from the Modern King James Version.

Chapter 1: A Thriving Deception

I selected from Greek mythology the story of the Trojan Horse, which is debated as an actual historical event. Whether it is a myth or a historical event, I believe it gives a clear illustration of a cunning and deceptive ploy between the Greek army and the city of Troy. What appeared to be a gift was in fact, a deadly weapon that brought about the destruction of the city of Troy.

In the best-known version, after a fruitless 10-year siege, the Greeks finally succeeded due to a devious strategy. The Greeks, under the guidance of Odysseus, who crafted the plan, built a huge wooden horse, which was the symbol of the city of Troy. He left it at the gates of the city, and then pretended to sail away, giving the impression that they had given up the fight. The Trojans believed that the huge wooden horse was a peace offering to their gods, and, thus, a symbol of their final victory after the long siege. They pulled the giant wooden horse into the middle of the city. That night, the Greek forces, hidden within, crept out and opened the gates for the rest of the Greek army, which had sailed back under cover of night. The Greek army entered the city and destroyed it.

Religion, as defined by Webster's, is the service and worship of God, or of the supernatural, a cause, a principle, or a system of beliefs held to with fervor and faith. There are many religions in the world. They range from witchcraft, which is the worship of the devil, to those which, perhaps, are not witchcraft per se but are still within the satanic kingdom of darkness. All religions other than Christianity are false religions. Sadly, even within Christianity, there are segments that are merely religious and not truly Christian.

When speaking of religion, I am addressing a supposed means of salvation by the practice of religious good works. The reality is that there is only one true way of salvation. No one can earn their salvation no matter how good their works may be or what sacrifices are made. To those who profess to be Christians by such means do not clearly understand the scriptures. There is only one way to salvation, and no mere religious practice, no matter how it may seem to be righteous, can possibly grant salvation. The scriptures are very clear about this matter. True Christianity is based on the person and teachings of Jesus of Nazareth and the Bible as the infallible and divine Word of God. Listed below are just a few of the scriptures that state unconditionally that there is no salvation other than through Jesus.

John 14:6 Jesus said to him, "I am the Way, the Truth, and the Life; no one comes to the Father but by Me."

Act 4:12 And there is salvation in no other One; for there is no other name under Heaven given among men by which we must be saved.

John 3:16 For God so loved the world that He gave His only-begotten Son, that whoever believes in Him should not perish but have everlasting life.

The bottom line between Christianity, as a mere form of religion, and true Christianity is the reality that there is only one possible means of salvation, and the heart of true Christianity is based on a personal relationship with God, and not on mere religious practices. In the following scripture Jesus is speaking to Nicodemus, who came to Jesus by night, sneaking off to see the man behind the miracles. Nicodemus was a powerful Pharisee and a member of the Sanhedrin, the Jewish ruling council. His inquiries into the miracles and ministry of Jesus produced the following response from Jesus.

John 3:1 And there was a man of the Pharisees named Nicodemus, a ruler of the Jews. **2** He came to Jesus by night and said to Him, Rabbi, we know that you are a teacher come from God; for no *man* can do these miracles which you do unless God is with him. **3** Jesus answered and said to him, Truly, truly, I say to you, Unless a man is born again, he cannot see the kingdom of God. **4** Nicodemus said to Him, How can a man be born when he is old? Can he enter the second *time* into his mother's womb and be born?

Nicodemus, a devout religious Jew, did not understand or comprehend what Jesus was saying, which is obvious from his inquiry. He asked, "How could a man be born when he is old? Can he enter a second time into his mother's womb and be born." Jesus' response was clear and repeated the heart of the matter, "You must be born again." The following scriptures are clear.

Matthew 7:21 Not everyone who says to Me, "Lord! Lord!" shall enter the kingdom of Heaven, but he who does the will of My Father in Heaven. **22** Many will say to Me in that day, Lord! Lord! Did we not prophesy in Your name, and through Your name throw out demons, and through Your name do many wonderful works? **23** And then I will say to them, I never knew you! Depart from Me, those working lawlessness!

This portion of scripture is alarming. Jesus did not say, "I once knew you, but you went away, so I no longer know you." He said, "I never knew you." They listed their religious works and assumed that their works were the means of salvation. They were shocked when they faced Jesus and He said, "I never knew you." Religious practices and all the good works one could possibly accumulate could never grant salvation.

The devil has offered a means by which we may supposedly enter into heaven, by working out our own salvation. We can determine our own terms. Religion, as the means of salvation, is the Trojan Horse of Christianity. Just as the people of Troy believed a lie, they believed that the battle had been won and collected their assumed trophy, which turned out to be their downfall. In the same way, religious practices alone give a false sense of salvation and security, but only produce death in the end. There are many different religions, and the real issue is religion as a means of salvation. This also applies to the religion of Christianity as well.

Such is the ploy of the enemy. Once again, religion, as a means of salivation, is the Trojan Horse of Christianity and the most cunning and effective ploy of the devil. The devil is not concerned at all about religion, in fact, he presents it as a gift. What makes religion a cunning and deceptive tool is when religion is substituted for a personal relationship with Jesus Christ. Jesus is the only means of salvation.

All the behavioral modification in the world will not result in salvation. No religious practice, no matter how pious, will ever grant the participants salvation. Jesus clearly states that to be saved, you must be born again. Being born again does not enroll you as a member of a religious order. Being born again gives you a relationship with the living God and makes you His child, literally born of God.

Chapter 2: Born Again

As stated in chapter one, there are many religions with extremely different beliefs, but they are not the reference of this book; however, we will be centering in on Christianity as a religion and some of its distorted beliefs. It is true that there are differing points of understanding and interpretation of scripture between Christian denominations, but it is my intention to steer clear of these areas as much as possible; however, it will be necessary to address some points of disagreement. No denomination has all the answers, and in some cases, what differs in our beliefs is not critical or essential to salvation. In other cases, the differences are critical and a matter of life or death. What is clear in scripture is that we, as believers in Christ, are not enemies, and the scriptures clearly declare who is our enemy. The following scripture is taken from Ephesians the sixth chapter, which describes spiritual warfare and identifies who our true enemy is.

Ephesians 6:12 For our struggle is not against flesh and blood, but against the rulers, against the authorities, against the powers of this dark world and against the spiritual forces of evil in the heavenly realms.

Our struggle is not against flesh and blood. The flesh and blood statement in Ephesians eliminates all humans since all humans are clearly flesh and blood. All those within denominations or other religions are also human and therefore flesh and blood, and therefore are not the enemies. No religious belief or doctrine can make one the enemy. Even if you were a member of a satanic cult, you are still not the enemy. You may work for and live for the enemy, but it does not make you the enemy. As Christians, our struggle is against rulers, authorities, powers of this dark world, and against the spiritual forces of evil in heavenly realms. These are all part of Satan's army, but he is the true enemy. It is sad that all of us allow the enemy to work through us at times and to different degrees, but being used by the enemy does not make us the enemy. It is clearly the evil one known as Satan, or Lucifer, who is the true enemy!

I titled this chapter, "Born Again." I did so since being born again is absolutely necessary if one is to be a Christian. If anyone is not born again, they are not now, nor will they ever be a Christian. Even within Christianity, the term *born again* is misunderstood or entirely disregarded.

In the first chapter, I shared some scriptures about Nicodemus, who was a high-ranking Jew within the separatist group known as the Pharisees. He was also a member of the Sanhedrin, an assembly of 71 elders appointed to sit as a tribunal in every city in the ancient Land of Israel. Whether he came to Jesus by night for cultural reasons, privacy purposes, curiosity, fear of reprisal from his Jewish peers, or simply out of respect for the Lord, he did so privately, within the cloak of night. Nicodemus made his way to their meeting place and would soon understand that being born again is God's requirement for entrance into heaven. The Lord knew the reason he came and recognized the spiritual need of this religious separatist. Even though he was a member of the Sanhedrin, a teacher of the law, and supposed himself to be a guardian of the truth, he did not know about the absolute essential element in being saved and entering into heaven. The following scripture gives us the beginning of the conversation between Nicodemus and Jesus.

John 3:2 He came to Jesus at night and said, "Rabbi, we know that you are a teacher who has come from God: for no one could perform the signs you are doing if God were not with him."

Jesus' response takes Nicodemus straight to the heart of the matter.

John 3:3 Jesus answered and said to him, "Truly, truly, I say to you, Unless a man is born again, he cannot see the kingdom of God."

We have his response in the following verse, which clearly shows that this spiritual leader, did not understand what Jesus meant by born again.

John 3:4 Nicodemus said to Him, How can a man be born when he is old? Can he enter the second *time* into his mother's womb and be born?" **5** Jesus answered, Truly, truly, I say to you, Unless a man is born of water and the Spirit, he cannot enter into the kingdom of God. **6** That which is born of the flesh is flesh, and that which is born of the Spirit is spirit. **7** Do not marvel that I said to you, You must be born again.

It is interesting that Jesus says to Nicodemus that he should not be surprised at His saying you must be born again. What was Jesus talking about? He did give him an answer, but it was obviously not an answer he understood.

Why must we be born again? How can we be born again? What does it mean to be born again? We need to go back to the beginning of time to understand. There is one thing that is essential to our understanding if we are to comprehend what it means to be born again. Foundational to our understanding is the reality that we are created as spirit beings. Adam was formed from the dust of the earth, and God breathed the Spirit of life into him, and he became a spiritual being. Adam's body was already created, but it was not alive. We see from the following scripture that something else was necessary for Adam to live.

Genesis 2:7 Then the Lord God formed a man from the dust of the ground and breathed into his nostrils the breath of life, and the man became a living being.

Adam, the first human created, was created a spirit being, and every other human that has existed was also born a spirit being and will exist forever. No one ever stops existing. Our bodies die, but we are immortal spirit beings, and therefore we will exist forever. The real issue is not existing eternally but where we will exist. There are literally millions of people who call themselves Christians and yet have never been born again, even though it is clear that Jesus said *you must be born again*. Once again, there is no other way to be a part of God's kingdom without being born again. It is essential that we understand what was lost in the garden of Eden and how that affected every person after that.

Adam and Eve were perfect and without flaw. They walked with God in the garden in the cool of the evening. There was no separation between them and God, and they were not only able to see Him, but they had fellowship with Him daily. What changed? Why were they separated from God and put out of the Garden of Eden? Well, they were not the first to be separated from God. There was an archangel named Lucifer, who was cast out of heaven to the earth. He was separated from God and cast out of heaven because of pride and attempting to put himself above God. The enemy of God was present in the Garden of Eden.

We need to go back to the beginning and see what happened in the Garden of Eden. We will find our answers in Genesis, the first book of the Bible, and the second and third chapters. I want to basically take it verse by verse so that from the scriptures, it will be clear just what occurred and what it meant.

Genesis chapter 2:8 Now the Lord God had planted a garden in the east, in Eden; and there he put the man he had formed. **9** The Lord God made all kinds of trees grow out of the ground—trees that were pleasing to the eye and good for food. In the middle of the garden were the tree of life and the tree of the knowledge of good and evil. **15** The Lord God took the man and put him in the Garden of Eden to work it and take care of it. **16** And the Lord God commanded the man, "You are free to eat from any tree in the garden; **17** but you must not eat from the tree of the knowledge of good and evil, for when you eat from it you will certainly die." **18** The Lord God said, "It is not good for the man to be alone. I will make a helper suitable for him." **19** Now the Lord God had formed out of the ground all the wild animals and all the birds in the sky. He brought them to the man to see what he would name them; and whatever the man called each living creature, that was its name. **20** So the man gave names to all the livestock, the birds in the sky, and all the wild animals. But for Adam no suitable helper was found. **21** So the Lord God caused the man to fall into a deep sleep; and while he was sleeping, he took one of the man's ribs and then closed up the place with flesh. **22** Then the Lord God made a woman from the rib he had taken out of the man, and he brought her to the man. **23** The man said, "This is now bone of my bones and flesh of my flesh; she shall be called 'woman,' for she was taken out of man."

So God created a garden and caused all manner of trees to grow that were pleasing to the eye and good for food. Then, in the middle of the Garden of Eden, he placed two special trees. First was the tree of life, and the other was the tree of the knowledge of good and evil. These were very significant and essential trees. They were free to eat from the trees in the garden, but He restricted one tree that they were not to eat from, or they would die. We will discuss this shortly. Then God had Adam name all the living creatures. God said it was not good for Adam to be alone as he had no mate, so God took a rib out of Adam's side and created a woman. Eve was not created from the dust of the earth but from a rib that came from Adam. She is the only human that came from man. After this, all humans, male or female, came from women. It is true that the seed was necessary from man, but no other human being came from the body of a man.

Now to the heart of the issue. Why the two special trees in the center of the garden, and why was one prohibited? The answer goes to the heart and intent of God in creating them. God wanted a family, and He created a means for the world to be populated and even commanded the man and woman to multiply and fill the earth. His heart was obviously for a large family. When we are born again, we become children of God, and He becomes our father. This is the basis of understanding that God desired a family. Jesus, in response to the disciples' request that He teach them how to pray, began with the instruction that they should start their prayers with our Father who art in Heaven. But why the tree of the knowledge of good and evil? God knew that to have a relationship with man, that man must have the ability to choose to do so. It could never be a one-sided relationship as that is not a relationship at all. God could have created them without free will and not given them a choice. They could have been created as robots. However, He gave them the ability to choose because, without the ability to choose, which is called *volition or free will,* there could be no relationship. Relationship requires two basic things. First, free will and then trust. The ability to choose was given, and trust would need to be built even though in reality, God had given them no reason to not trust Him. I could hold a gun to your head and ask if you want to be my friend, and in all probability, your answer would be yes. That would not make you my friend. Without a choice, there could be no friendship or relationship. Trust is also a necessary ingredient to a relationship. God did not force them to do as He said, or else, neither did He give them any reason not to trust Him. In fact, He trusted them by giving them dominion over all the earth. One would think from their daily walks with God that they would have trusted Him. He gave them absolutely no reason for not trusting Him. The choice was clearly theirs. They could trust Him and follow His instructions about the tree of the knowledge of good and evil, and they would not have died. Who knows what the outcome would have been had they obeyed God. The penalty of eating of the tree of the knowledge of good and evil was death. It is important to understand that God did not say, do not eat of the tree of the knowledge of good and evil, or I will kill you. It was not a threat; it was a warning about the danger involved in eating from that tree. It is not clear how many trees there were and what the variety was, but it is clear that there was only one restriction out of all the trees that were created for them. In all that God created for them and blessed them with, there was only one restriction. They could have avoided ever experiencing death. If God had not given them life, they would never have had a choice, and they could never have had a true relationship with God without the ability to choose.

What happened? Why did they mistrust God and eventually eat of the tree of death? The enemy was at work. Perhaps if the enemy had not been in the garden, they might not have ever been tempted to eat from the tree. We don't know how long the devil worked on Eve, it could have been a month, a year, or even longer. I'm surprised that she never discussed it with God. She could have easily said that she was talking with the serpent, and he said, etc. It makes me wonder what their walks together did for the relationship. It is apparent that in the end, Eve did not trust God, nor do we know if she ever did. We also do not know if Adam was ever a part of the discussions between Eve and Lucifer. What we do know is that she listened and ate of the tree and gave some to Adam, and he ate also. What we do have from Genesis, the third chapter, is a record of the discussion the enemy and Eve had concerning the tree.

Chapter 3:1 Now the serpent was more crafty than any of the wild animals the Lord God had made. He said to the woman, "Did God really say, 'You must not eat from any tree in the garden'?" **2** The woman said to the serpent, "We may eat fruit from the trees in the garden. **3** But God did say, 'You must not eat fruit from the tree that is in the middle of the garden, and you must not touch it, or you will die.'" **4** "You will not certainly die," the serpent said to the woman. **5** "For God knows that when you eat from it, your eyes will be opened, and you will be like God, knowing good and evil." **6** When the woman saw that the fruit of the tree was good for food and pleasing to the eye, and also desirable for gaining wisdom, she took some and ate it. She also gave some to her husband, who was with her, and he ate it. **7** Then the eyes of both of them were opened, and they realized they were naked; so they sewed fig leaves together and made coverings for themselves.

We know that the tempter was Satan and not a snake. We have no record of a snake or any other animal speaking, and no animal has ever had the ability to do so. Why he picked the snake is not known. It is interesting that the snake was said to be more crafty than any of the wild animals. Crafty and cunning are characteristics of Satan and may have been a reason for his choosing the snake as it was most like him. Apparently, at this time Eve had no fear of the snake, and evidently, the snake walked upright.

The first step was to put a seed of doubt in the mind of Eve as to what God said and His motive for doing so. He said, "Did God really say, 'You must not eat from any tree in the garden?" God really did say they were not to eat of one specific tree, but not all trees. Eve's response was, "We may eat fruit from the trees in the garden, but God did say, 'You must not eat fruit from the tree that is in the middle of the garden, and you must not touch it, or you will die.'" The scriptures do not say that Eve heard directly from God, but God did tell Adam directly. Adam must have told Eve what God had said, and he may have added that they were not to touch it. Whatever the reason, Eve's statement was a distortion of what God had actually said. God did not say you cannot touch it.

The two factors required for a relationship are free will and trust, and it is exactly what the lies and the attack of the enemy were centered on. First, the enemy focused Eve's attention to that which was withheld, the one prohibition. He does not ask if God said they could not eat of the one tree, but of all the trees, which was clearly a distortion of what God had said and what God's intent for the tree was. In light of the beautiful garden and all the trees that they could eat from, Eve now focuses on the one tree they are not to eat from. Eve must have wondered, why did God tell them not to eat of this tree? Why would He withhold the fruit of this one tree? Why was it so special? We can see his answer from the following scripture.

Genesis 3:5, For God knows that in the day you eat of it, then your eyes shall be opened, and you shall be as God, knowing good and evil.

Next, Satan outright calls God a liar. He boldly states, "You will not certainly die." At this point, she had to be wondering why God would lie to her. Why would she believe the snake and not the God who created them and gave them a beautiful garden to live in as well as a number of trees they could freely eat from? He suggested that God did not really want what was best for Adam and Eve but rather was withholding something from them that was essentially good. The next scripture totally puzzles me. Her response to Satan's deception and lies is recorded in the following scripture.

Genesis 3:6 And when the woman saw that the tree was good for food, and that it was pleasing to the eyes, and a tree to be desired to make wise, she took of its fruit and ate. She also gave to her husband with her, and he ate

Really, she now sees the tree of death as good for food, pleasing to the eye, and desirable for gaining wisdom, but instead of gaining wisdom, she acted foolishly. Her seeing the tree as being good for food and pleasing to the eye exhibits her out-and-out deception. Adam knew very well what God had said, and yet when Eve gave him the fruit, he ate it. Perhaps she had been talking with him all along about what the serpent was saying. The Hebrew word translated "crafty" (*'arum*) does not mean wicked as much as wise. Eve's sin was not so much an act of great wickedness as it was an act of great folly. She already had all the good she needed and indeed more than she needed, but she wanted more. The bottom line was that she wanted to rule her own life. Their sin brought about a number of drastic changes. The immediate effects of sin and the resulting curses are listed in the following verses of Genesis chapter 3.

Genesis 3:14 And Jehovah God said to the serpent, Because you have done this you *are* cursed more than all cattle, and more than every animal of the field. You shall go upon your belly, and you shall eat dust all the days of your life. **15** And I will put enmity between you and the woman, and between your seed and her Seed;

He will bruise your head, and you shall bruise His heel. **16** To the woman He said, I will greatly increase your sorrow and your conception. In pain, you shall bear sons, and your desire shall be toward your husband, and he shall rule over you. **17** And to Adam He said, Because you have listened to the voice of your wife and have eaten of the tree, of which I commanded you, saying, You shall not eat *of* it! The ground *is* cursed for your sake. In pain shall you eat of it all the days of your life. **18** It shall also bring forth thorns and thistles to you, and you shall eat the herb of the field. **19** In the sweat of your face, you shall eat bread until you return to the ground, for out of it you were taken. For dust you *are*, and to dust you shall return.

Verse 14 gives us the answer to the snake apparently walking upright, as the curse was that snakes would now crawl on their bellies. Verse 15 gives us the word enmity to describe the relationship between the snake and the woman. *Enmity* means a deep-seated hatred. Verse 16 shows that the pains in child birth are attributed to Eve's disobedience. The woman was taken from the man and was to be a helpmeet, which was a suitable helper and spouse. The relationship between them was changed in that now the woman's desire would be for her husband. The desire was not a pleasant desire but a craving for a man. She also went from a helper to a subordinate. Although she was tempted by Satan and sinned, she is the one who tempted her husband to sin. Verse 17 attaches the curse of the ground to Adam, and not because he obeyed the leading of the serpent, but because he listened to his wife and ate fruit from the tree that God had commanded him not to eat. Adam and Eve were not cursed. It was the snake and the ground that was cursed. Adam's care of the garden was now going to be difficult, and through painful toil, he would eat from it all the days of his life. By the sweat of your brow, you will eat your food, and you will return to the dust from which you were taken.

So what does this have to do with us and being born again? I stated earlier that we are created as spirit beings. Adam had a body that was formed by God, but it was lifeless. It was not until God breathed into his nostrils the breath of life that Adam became a living being. Adam's lifeless body was not Adam but a body he would live in. The body was created from the dust of the earth, but the spirit was from God.

Genesis 2:7 Then the Lord God formed a man from the dust of the ground and breathed into his nostrils the breath of life, and the man became a living being.

Genesis 1:27 So God created mankind in his own image, in the image of God he created them; male and female he created them.

We do not know what form God had as He met and walked with Adam and Eve in the garden. We do know that God is a spirit being. Adam's being created in God's image was not a matter of having a body; it was a matter of having the Spirit of God breathed into Him. Adam was created in the image of God, which means he was created as a spirit being, as God is a spirit being. The body of Adam was created by God from the dust of the earth and was lifeless. God breathed the breath of life into Adam, and he became a living being. A spirit being.

John 4:24 God *is* a spirit, and they who worship Him must worship in spirit and in truth.

Adam and Eve knew no evil. They were absolutely innocent. We can see their innocence from the following scripture.

Genesis 2:25 And they were both naked, the man and his wife; and they were not ashamed.

We can see a dramatic change in them as soon as they ate of the tree of the knowledge of good and evil.

Genesis 3:7 And the eyes of both of them were opened. And they knew that they *were* naked. And they sewed fig leaves together and made girdles for themselves. **8** And they heard the voice of Jehovah God walking in the garden in the cool of the day. And

Adam and his wife hid themselves from the presence of Jehovah God in the middle of the trees of the garden. **9** And Jehovah God called to Adam and said to him, Where *are* you? **10** And he said, I heard Your voice in the garden, and I was afraid, because I *am* naked, and I hid myself. **11** And He said, Who told you that you *were* naked? Have you eaten of the tree which I commanded you that you should not eat?

They immediately lost their innocence and were aware of their nakedness. Also, fear entered into them and they hid themselves from God. God certainly knew why they were hiding and asked the question to confront their disobedience. We do not know what they may have thought God would do in response to their disobedience, but now fear entered into the relationship. God acted in mercy toward them and made skin coverings for them to hide their nakedness.

They did not die in the sense of no longer existing but continued to exist, and neither of them died physically at that time. In fact, Adam existed on earth for 930 years; however, we do not know how old Eve was when she was no longer on the earth. What does it mean then that if they ate of the tree they would die? They were both created in the image of God, and that clearly meant that they were without sin, as God has no sin. As soon as sin entered into them from eating the forbidden fruit, they no longer had a pure or divine nature as sin changed their very nature. The death was not the death of a spiritual being created to exist forever, as all spirit beings will exist forever. Their relationship with God was not the same. Their very nature changed, from a spiritual nature to a fallen nature. The death they incurred was the relationship they had with God, and they were now spiritually separated from God. The walks in the garden no longer happened, and they were put out of the garden.

Geneses 3:22 And the LORD God said, "The man has now become like one of us, knowing good and evil. He must not be allowed to reach out his hand and take also from the tree of life and eat and live forever." **23** So the LORD God banished him from the Garden of Eden to work the ground from which he had been taken. **24** After He drove the man out, He placed on the east side of the Garden of Eden cherubim and a flaming sword flashing back and forth to guard the way to the tree of life.

This does not mean that they were like God now, only in the sense that they were now aware of evil of which they were not aware of until after eating from the tree of the knowledge of good and evil. It is clear that there were two trees in the center of the garden. The tree of the knowledge of good and evil and the tree of life. We do not know what would have happened if they had eaten of the tree of life. We do know that they ate of the tree of knowledge of good and evil and therefore, they had to be protected from eating from the tree of life to prevent them from eternal life in a sinful condition. Sin had separated them from the pure state of innocence and communion with God, and God never intended them to live forever in sin. We do not know what would have happened if they had eaten of the tree of life instead of the tree of the knowledge of good and evil. Would the test be passed on to their offspring, or perhaps the tree the knowledge of good and evil would have been removed? The choice was no longer based on the two trees. God still communicated with them but not on the same basis as it was before the fall.

The fallen nature was passed down through the generations through the male seed and had nothing to do with the goodness or behavior of the offspring. The fallen nature was not a matter of choice but a matter of inheritance. We all inherited the fallen nature and were born separated from God. This is why we must be born again. Jesus came in the flesh to pay for the sins of all those who would receive Him as savior. He was born of a virgin and not from a man but of the Holy Spirit. He did not have a fallen nature as he was not born from a man's seed. He was both God and man. The following scripture declares the following in response to Mary's question as to how she could possibly be having a baby when she had not been with any man but was a virgin.

Luke 1:34 "How will this be," Mary asked the angel, "since I am a virgin?" **35** The angel answered, "The Holy Spirit will come on you and the power of the Most High will overshadow you. So the holy one to be born will be called the Son of God.

Understanding that there is a difference between a natural birth between a man and a woman and a spiritual birth born of the Spirit of God is essential to the reality that we must be born again. The apostle John, under the influence of the Holy Spirit, wrote the following statement concerning this.

John 3:6 That which is born of the flesh is flesh, and that which is born of the Spirit is spirit. **7** Do not marvel that I said to you, You must be born again.

We are all born of the flesh through our parents. We must be born of the Spirit to be born again. This is a miracle that changes our very nature. We are a new creation. We are God's children. We are once again created in His image as Adam and Eve were in the beginning. That means we can have a relationship with God and walk with Him in this life and communicate with Him as well. We are no longer separated from Him!

2 Corinthians 5:17 So that if any one *is* in Christ, *that one is* a new creature; old things have passed away; behold, all things have become new.

Many people believe that they are God's children, but they are not. Many people say we are all children of God and we are all created in His image. If you are not born again, you are not a child of God. In fact, if you are not born again, you are a child of the devil. This is not by choice but by inheritance.

John 8:44 You are of the devil as father, and the lusts of your father you will do. He was a murderer from the beginning, and did not abide in the truth because there is no truth in him. When he speaks a lie, he speaks of his own, for he is a liar and the father of it.

It is not that we are deserving of God's love and forgiveness, but we must accept the provision God made through the death and resurrection of Jesus if we are to be born again. It is by His grace, which stands for unmerited favor, that we are saved and born again. The following portion of scripture states this truth.

Ephesians 2:1 And He has made you alive, who were once dead in trespasses and sins, **2** in which you once walked according to the course of this world, according to the prince of the power of the air, the spirit that now works in the children of disobedience; **3** among whom we also had our way of life in times past, in the lusts of our flesh, fulfilling the desires of the flesh and of the thoughts, and were by nature the children of wrath, even as others. **4** But God, who is rich in mercy, for His great love with which He loved us, **5** (even when we were dead in sins) has made us alive together with Christ (by grace you are saved), **6** and has raised us up together and made us sit together in the heavenlies in Christ Jesus, **7** so that in the ages to come He might show the exceeding riches of His grace in His kindness toward us through Christ Jesus. **8**

For by grace you are saved through faith, and that not of yourselves, it is the gift of God, **9** not of works, lest anyone should boast. **10** For we are His workmanship, created in Christ Jesus to good works, which God has before ordained that we should walk in them.

When I was born again, I received eternal life and not eternal existence, which I already had. My eternal existence would have been in hell, eternally separated from God and suffering the penalty forever. Once I was born again, I received spiritual life and was then in fellowship with the Lord, and I became His child. Jesus paid the price for my sins and all my sins have been forgiven. I can now have fellowship with Him and I am a new person. The old man died, and there was a new man created by God, and this is the realty of being born again.

Adam and Eve did not have a clue that their disobedience would adversely affect all the generations that followed. We did not make that choice, they did, but we inherited the results of their choice. What they had in the garden was lost until Jesus came and made a way for us to return to the garden.

Chapter 3: Misrepresentation of the Gospel

What is the gospel? The Greek word used in the scriptures for the gospel is also interpreted as the "good news" and refers to what was accomplished by Jesus Christ's birth, death, and resurrection. Jesus paid the price for our salvation, our new birth into His family, and the restoration of our fellowship with the Father.

In many cases, what was truly good news has been distorted. By distortion, I mean presenting a misleading or false account or impression. In chapter 1, we saw the scriptural truths, proving that religious practices are not and can never be a means of salvation. In chapter 2, we saw from the scriptures that salvation could not be achieved through religious practices and that it was absolutely clear that we must be born again. Salvation through religious practices is a distortion of the gospel. In this chapter, I desire to examine some of the distortions of the gospel.

It is not my intent to be mean or unkind in any way, and it would certainly be wrong of me to be judgmental or condemning; however, it is important that I explain some of the distortions of the gospel. I know that God is able to draw anyone unto Himself and save them without any other person being involved. It is not a matter of ineptness on God's part, as He is the only one who can truly save. Still, we are part of God's family and, as such, commissioned to share the gospel. Before Jesus ascended into heaven, He gave His disciples some specific instructions. One of the well-known instructions to His disciples is called the great commission. We, as born-again believers, are His disciples. We are part of His Kingdom and are called to share the gospel with the lost and disciple those who are saved. The following scripture gives us Jesus' commission to all true believers.

Matthew 28:18 And Jesus came and spoke to them, saying, All authority is given to Me in Heaven and in earth. **19** Therefore go and teach all nations, baptizing them in the name of the Father and of the Son and of the Holy Spirit, **20** teaching them to observe all things, whatever I commanded you. And, behold, I am with you all the days until the end of the world. Amen.

Since we are commissioned to share the gospel, it is vitally important that we, as born-again believers, share the true gospel and not some distortion. For instance, the message that God loves us and that Jesus died on the cross for all who would receive Him is absolutely true and clear. However, in chapter 1, we saw that religion was substituted for this truth and that religion was a means of salvation.

I have heard many Christians, as well as some pastors, make the following statement, "we are all sinners saved by grace." It may be from a misunderstanding of the scriptures, or perhaps because they do not want to appear to be haughty that the statement is made; however, the statement is not true for born-again believers. We were sinners prior to salvation, and we were certainly saved by grace, but at the point of salvation, we are no longer sinners but saints. Our very nature has been changed, and we are now children of God and saints. The New Testament scriptures are full of Christians being called saints. So, what does saint mean? In its most basic sense, a saint is a "holy one," someone who is set apart for God's special purposes.

As a result, a born-again believer is a saint. I, as a born-again Christian, am no longer a sinner saved by grace. I was a sinner, and I was saved by grace, but now I am a saint who, at times, sorry to say, sins. I do not lose my salvation over sins, and Jesus provided for us the means by which we can ask forgiveness for the sins we commit as saints, and they will be forgiven. What I finally discovered was that I needed to pray for deliverance from sins, as Jesus broke the power of sin over our lives. Why should I pray over and over again for forgiveness for the same sins? Why not pray for deliverance? A holy life is expected of the saints, and

Jesus provided the means for living such a life. I do not believe that this distortion is intentional, but it is still a distortion of the scriptures. I am holy because He made me holy, and I did not become holy through behavioral modification, although I am to live a holy life by the power of God working in my life.

The following scenario is based on my background and what I have witnessed many times. It is what I grew up seeing and understanding as the presentation of the gospel and the invitation to receive Jesus as savior. The typical salvation message was all that was required for salvation was to repeat a prayer, usually prayed by the pastor, and that's it. To be fair, the salvation message was not always the same and, in some cases, more complete and accurate.

Although this varies within different denominations, I grew up with the following scenario. The precursor to the prayer was that all the congregation was to bow their heads and close their eyes, with no one looking around. Then everyone in the congregation was requested to pray the simple salvation prayer along with anyone who may have raised their hand for salvation. We did not know if anyone actually raised their hand, unless of course we were looking around. This was a prayer asking forgiveness for sins and that Jesus would come into their heart. I personally refused to pray along as I was saved and did not need to ask Jesus to save me and come into my heart. I have the Holy Spirit living within me! I believe this is done from a sincere desire to not embarrass a potential new believer. My question is, why should they be embarrassed? Why would we teach them that accepting Jesus is embarrassing? What is going on in heaven when a sinner comes to Christ? The following portion of scripture gives a good picture of what is going on in heaven.

Luke 15:4 What man of you, having a hundred sheep, if he loses one of them, does not leave the ninety-nine in the wilderness and go after that which is lost until he finds it? **5** And when he has found *it*, he lays *it* on his shoulders, rejoicing. **6** And when he comes home, he calls together *his* friends and neighbors, saying to them, Rejoice with me, for I have found my sheep which was lost. **7** I say to you that likewise, joy shall be in Heaven over one sinner who repents, more than over ninety-nine just persons who need no repentance.

Can you picture all of heaven rejoicing in the salvation of one soul? Why are we not doing the same? In most cases, we don't even know if anyone raised their hand. What if they leave thinking they are saved and, indeed, are not saved? We have told them that all they have to do is repeat a little prayer, and they are saved and good to go. What about discipleship? I am not saying that God cannot work with that person and if they are not truly saved, still bring them to salvation, but let's consider the following portions of scripture when we are speaking of salvation and repentance. Jesus is the one speaking, and He is not explaining how they should repeat a little prayer after Him.

Luke 9:23 And He said to all, If anyone desires to come after Me, let him deny himself and take up his cross daily and follow Me. **24** For whoever will save his life shall lose it, but whoever will lose his life for My sake, he shall save it. **25** For what is a man profited if he gains the whole world and loses himself, or is cast away? **26** For whoever shall be ashamed of Me and of My Words, the Son of Man shall be ashamed of him when He shall come in His own and *in His* Father's glory, and that of the holy angels.

True salvation results in true repentance. Repentance is not just asking forgiveness, but it is a change of mind and direction; living a different life is expected. In the Bible, the word *repentance* literally means the act of changing one's mind. True biblical repentance goes beyond remorse, regret, or feeling bad about one's sin. It involves more than merely turning away from sin. In its fullest sense, it is a term for a complete change of direction involving a judgment upon the past and a deliberate redirection

31

for the future. One cannot be saved by changing one's behavior, but changing one's behavior is the expected process accompanying true salvation. Feeling embarrassed or ashamed should never be attached to a presentation of the gospel. We should agree wholeheartedly with the Apostle Paul as he declares the following.

Romans 1:16 For I am not ashamed of the gospel of Christ, for it is *the* power of God unto salvation to everyone who believes, to the Jew first and also to the Greek.

Another approach that is used at times in an attempt to keep the unsaved out of hell is to try and scare hell out of them by describing what hell is like and that they are facing an angry God. Or they are told that they better get their act together or they will go to hell. If they could truly get their act together, they would not need the Lord and His grace working in their lives. Could they possibly be saved by changing their behavior? No, behavior modification cannot save anyone. Does either of these sound like good news? Did God really intend to threaten people with hell. I know that hell is a reality, and I know that I don't want anyone to go to hell, and God does not want anyone to go to hell, either. The following scripture declares God's desire in this matter.

2 Peter 3:9 The Lord is not slow concerning His promise, as some count slowness, but is long-suffering toward us, not purposing that any should perish, but that all should come to repentance.

Matthew 25:41 Then He also shall say to those on *the* left *hand*, Depart from Me, you cursed, into everlasting fire prepared for the devil and his angels.

The Judgment Day and hell are real; however, hell was not created for us, but for the devil and his cohorts. The unsaved, as children of the devil will also be with him in hell, but they do not have to be. Accepting the salvation provided for us and being born again is the only way of escaping this; nevertheless, it is not God's will or His desire for us to go to hell!

Fear is a tool of the devil and fear is not from God. To preach fear is not a proper presentation of the gospel. Fear is not faith, and we are saved by grace through faith and not fear. We are to fear God, but the fear of God is a reverence for God and not a terror. Indeed, the scriptures teach that perfect love casts out all fear.

1 John 4:18 There is no fear in love, but perfect love casts out fear, because fear has torment. He who fears has not been perfected in love.

Therefore, presenting God as a God to be in terror of is not a biblical truth and is not true to the heart of God. It is a fact that all of us were born into sin and have followed the devil to varying degrees, and the Bible declares that all have sinned and come short of the glory of God. I would not want to be one of those on His left, but as a born-again Christian, I do not have to fear hell, because I will not be going there.

Another distortion of the good news, the gospel, is that God wants all Christians to be rich and healthy. Health and wealth are strong emphases in a number of denominations. There are some major distortions of the scriptures within this so-called gospel. I am not sure where I want to go from here in this area as it is extensive, but I will point out a couple of areas that are really both scary and an abomination. Online, as an extension of their ministries, are those who actually declare they can pray for a healing and you will be healed if you send in a faith gift of the declared amount. They unashamedly declare that if you send them this faith gift, they will pray for you, and God will heal you. Many will even give a numerical scriptural reference as a sign of what amount should be sent in by faith to get their healing. Why would God hear their prayer and heal? Why would He not hear your prayers and heal you? Also, great abundance is promised for gifts to their ministry, with the proof of their claims being all the money they have. If you give to them, you will also be rich. Who did they give to? They must have had some blessed ministry, and as they gave to them, they got wealthy also. Who is our provider anyway? Isn't Jehovah Jireh our provider? I do believe that those who preach and teach such things are described by Jesus in the following portion of scripture.

Luke 16:13 No servant can serve two masters. For either he will hate the one and love the other, or else he will hold to the one and despise the other. You cannot serve God and mammon.

In Greek, the word for mammon is riches personified and opposed to God. *You either are serving God or some personification called mammon.* The dictionary description for personify is: to attribute a personal nature or human characteristics to something not human. Even billionaires who have served mammon all their lives cannot depend on their assumed god, mammon, to save them when they are diagnosed with incurable cancer.

I certainly do believe from scripture that God wants us to have an abundant life, but that does not mean extreme wealth. I'm not saying that God does not bless with finances and that in giving one does receive back; however, not every believer is wealthy, nor is it God's plan for every Christian to be so. When people preach that if you give to their ministry, you will receive back wealth, as they have done in their ministry, I wonder where the heart is and if it is not clearly opposed to God. In essence, money (mammon) is declared to be the provider of healing and provision. Who can purchase a healing, and quite frankly, what good is all the money in the world if you are sick and dying? You might be able to get the very best doctors, but they are also limited in what they can do. I know that my God has provided for my family these past fifty years as we have walked with Him. We, like many other Christians, are not wealthy, but God is our provider, and He has been faithful.

Enough said about false misrepresentations of the gospel. What is important is to know the real gospel, the amazing good news brought to us from heaven by God Himself. Probably the most quoted scripture that goes to the heart of the gospel is the following;

John 3:16 For God so loved the world that He gave His only-begotten Son, that whoever believes in Him should not perish but have everlasting life.

The scriptures state clearly that God is love, and no matter what people may think or believe, God is love. Does God love you? Yes, He does! What is absolutely amazing is that God did not just declare He was love; He demonstrated His love for us in a way that is almost beyond comprehension. We have discussed in earlier chapters that we were alienated from God and that having a relationship with Him and knowing Him personally was impossible. We inherited this condition, and it was this condition that had to be dealt with. It seems to me that God could have just forgiven all and let it go. The reality is that God is also just. The penalty for sin had to be paid if we were ever to be able to have a relationship with Him. What could possibly satisfy the justice of God and open the door to communion with Him? The answer was the sacrifice of His son Jesus. The scripture says that without the shedding of blood, there can be no remission of sin. Remission is the cancellation of a debt, charge, or penalty. Not only was there a sacrifice needed, but it had to be one that would cancel the penalty of our sin by truly paying the price. God did not have a choice in this if He wanted us redeemed, as there was only one worthy to pay the price. Jesus was not forced to be our redeemer, it was His love for His Father and for us that caused Him to willingly choose to do what His Father asked.

God loves you and wants a relationship with you. This is the gospel, the good news! He is not mad at you or vindictive against you. He manifested the depth of His love for us when He sent His son to pay for our sins and open the door for us to be His children. God has a plan for your life, and who could possibly pick a better plan than God? He wants to know you and daily walk with you, and finally spend all eternity with you in a place He has prepared for all His children, a place called heaven. Jesus, as He was preparing to leave this world, said the following words to His disciples, which includes us as His disciples.

John 14:1 Let not your heart be troubled. You believe in God, believe also in me. **2** In My Father's house are many mansions; if *it were* not *so*, I would have told you. I go to prepare a place for you. **3** And if I go and prepare a place for you, I will come again and receive you to Myself, so that where I am, you may be also.

1 Corinthians 2:9 But as it is written, "Eye has not seen, nor ear heard," nor has it entered into the heart of man, "the things which God has prepared for those who love Him."

Hebrews 4:13 Neither is there any creature that is not manifest in His sight, but all things *are* naked and opened to the eyes of Him with whom we have to do.

God knows where you are. It does not take some fancy prayer or special process to get to Him and to be saved. Religion may have their forms for service times, and those may vary, but that is fine, but that is not what I am talking about. You could be in a prison in Iran, and God could reach you there. There is no sin He cannot forgive, and He already paid the price for your salvation. I was high on drugs and suicidal, and knelt by my bed and prayed. "I have heard about you all my life and I do not know if you are real or not, but if you will show me that you are real, then you can have this life and do whatever you want with it." "If you are not real, then I will end my life as I can't live this way any longer." Without going into all the details, He did show me, and I did eventually keep my end of the bargain. At the writing of this book, I have been a born-again Christian for fifty years, and He has been faithful to me every day of that fifty years. He will be the same for you. I pray and hope with all my heart to see you in heaven.

Chapter 4: What's Up with Sin?

In my opinion, sin is one of the most misunderstood issues within Christianity. To really explain what I just said, I need to go back to the beginning, to the garden of Eden. The creation of the Garden and the elements within have already been discussed in the preceding chapters, but a brief review is necessary.

In the first chapter of the book of Genesis, we have the account of God creating the earth and all that was in it. He did not create it just to be creative or to have an earth. There was a purpose beyond the creation of earth. In the twenty-fifth verse, we have the record of God creating man. All that was created was given to Adam and Eve to rule over. Every need was provided for them. They had plenty to eat and a beautiful garden to live in. Greater than all of that was the fact that each day, in the cool of the evening, they walked with God.

He did not create them as robots but as human beings and gave them volition, the power of choice. Their choice was not limited to which fruit to eat, and in this case, the one fruit chosen had extremely grievous consequences. It would seem that they had it made, so why the ability to choose? They had fellowship with God but could not have a relationship with God without the ability to choose. Fellowship is defined as a friendly association, especially with people who share one's interests. I can have fellowship at church, and I do, but it does not mean I have a relationship with those I have fellowship with. Most of the time, we do not know much, if anything about them, except that they come to church. To have a relationship requires a choice to pursue one, and the choice obviously needs to be a mutual one. God knew that relationship required the ability to choose, and without trust there could be no real relationship. Choice and trust are two absolutely necessary ingredients for a relationship. It is sad, but whatever the walks in the garden did for Eve, they did not build trust in God.

What was the choice that would require them to trust God? It was to trust His warning. There were two trees in the center of the garden. We do not know how close they were in proximity, but we do know that both were in the center of the garden. One was not to be eaten from as it would cause death, and the other, if eaten, would give eternal life. The choice would seem to be a no-brainer. I can eat from any tree in the garden except this one tree. What a deal. Below is the scriptural warning God gave to Adam.

Genesis 2:16 and the Lord God commanded the man, "You are free to eat from any tree in the garden; **17** but you must not eat from the tree of the knowledge of good and evil, for when you eat from it you will certainly die."

God created the whole world for man. God's heart for family did not stop with Adam and Eve. God wanted a large family. We know this from His directions to Adam and Eve. He told them to multiply and fill the earth.

We know from the scriptures that the devil tempted Eve, and she ate of the tree of the knowledge of good and evil and gave some fruit to Adam, and he ate. So we have the record of the first sin.

The Greek word for sin, (hamartia) means to miss the mark. The Hebrew also means missing the mark or off the mark. Eating from the tree definitely missed the mark. God had commanded them not to eat of it and gave them a clear warning. Their disobedience brought about immediate consequences. They did not die physically, but their fellowship with God changed, and they realized they were naked. Fear entered in also, and they hid themselves in the garden. They were sewing together leaves from the garden for a covering when God called out to them. For the first time, sin had entered into the world and would be multiplied beyond comprehension. At the end of Genesis chapter 3, we find a rather interesting consequence. Adam and Eve are driven from the garden to keep them from potentially eating from the tree of life.

Genesis 3:24 And He drove out the man. And He placed cherubs at the east of the garden of Eden, and a flaming sword which turned every way, to guard the way to the tree of life.

Why would God want to be sure to keep them from the tree of life? If they had eaten from the tree after their disobedience, they would have lived forever in a fallen and sinful condition. Their disobedience not only effected their lives but the lives of all who came after them. I have often wondered how long it took to get Eve to eat of the tree, and how long the test would have continued had they not eaten from the tree when they did. What if they had not eaten of the tree of the knowledge of good and evil but instead had eaten of the tree of life? Would all who followed after have received the reward of their obedience? Would their obedience have caused God to remove the tree of the knowledge of good and evil from the garden so that all who followed could live forever in paradise? I don't believe it could have been so because God did not create man to own Him but gave Him the ability to choose, and I believe that choice was intended for all men, women, and children. Relationship is between at least two, and a relationship with God requires a choice. We each have the same choice Adam and Eve had. It is not about some fruit on a tree, but it is still about the heart of the matter. We can choose to trust Him and His Word and accept Him as our savior and Lord, or we can reject His offer. He has made the first move with each of us by providing the choice. He has made His choice! He loves us and wants a relationship with us.

The greatest tool the enemy has ever devised is what this book is all about. Religion has prevented and still is preventing literally millions of people from being born again and becoming God's children. I believe it is the greatest weapon he has ever devised. With those who are blindly following religion into hell, Satan's battle against them is already won. That leaves the enemy one target, God's children.

God did not create sin. Sin came into this world through temptation and a wrong choice. There was only one restriction in the entire garden that God created for them. That restriction was for the purpose of relationship, not testing or punishment. His desire was not to see if they would obey but to see if they would trust Him. If He just wanted obedience, He could have kept choice from them, and there would have been no possibility of disobedience. Relationship with us was and is the heart of God and the purpose for creating mankind. If He wanted to control them, He definitely could have. He did not threaten them; He warned them. If they had trusted Him, they would not have died.

Satan has no hope of defeating God, and he knows his days are numbered. No attack he could devise has any chance. However, Satan hates God, and the worst he can do against Him is to attack His children. If I hated someone, and thank God that I do not, the worst thing I could do against them is to do damage to their children. If someone does not attack me personally but attacks my children, am I not still being attacked? Even more so! Satan does not care at all about me personally; however, if he can get to me since I am a child of God, he can get to my Heavenly Father, and that is his real target. Fortunately, God has defeated him, and God is more than able to protect and defend his children against any attack.

So sin originated in the garden and was the product of deception. Sin is still the means by which the enemy steals what God has for us. He may now have more ways of tempting us as the means of doing so is greater through television, social media, and the internet, just to name a few. Technology has certainly opened a door for much easier access and a multitude of opportunities for temptation to sin.

The strategies of the enemy have not changed. God wanted a relationship which required choice and trust. The first and continued attack of the enemy was not directed at eating some fruit, it was all about trust. He starts with questioning and distorting what God said. I do not know how the enemy knew that the tree of the knowledge of good and evil was prohibited, but what I do know is that he started his deception by talking about the trees. Did God say you could not eat of every tree of the garden? His inquiry to Eve was to discover just how sure she was about what God had said.

Genesis 3:1 Now the serpent was more cunning than any beast of the field which Jehovah God had made. And he said to the woman, *Is it* so that God has said, You shall not eat of every tree of the garden? **2** And the woman said to the serpent, We may eat of the fruit of the trees of the garden. **3** But of the fruit of the tree which *is* in the middle of the garden, God has said, You shall not eat of it, neither shall you touch it, lest you die.

She must have known which tree it was? She simply says the tree in the middle of the garden. We know that there was at least two. Furthermore, in her response to the serpent, we can see that she adds to what God said because God said nothing about touching the tree. What God said was now being distorted from both sides, the enemies and Eve's.

Now the narrative changes from questioning what God had said to a direct rebuttal of what God had said. Satan declares, "you shall surely not die!" He moves from questioning God's motives to a clear declaration that God had lied to her. Amazing, the liar calling God a liar. His next question is still directed toward motive. Why would God lie to you about eating from this specific tree. We can see from the following scripture that he was definitely accusing God of withholding from her. Why was He withholding from her? He actually declares the truth. Certainly, he has the wrong motive for the truth and clothed in the lie that God's motive was to withhold.

Genesis 3:5 for God knows that in the day you eat of it, then your eyes shall be opened, and you shall be as God, knowing good and evil.

This verse and the next one are baffling to me. As I said before, we do not have the time lines nor the details of the conversations Satan had with Eve. How could she possibly believe that God was withholding from her when He gave her life, provided a mate for her, gave her a beautiful garden to live in, and an abundance of trees to eat from? God even gave them dominion over all He had created. It seems like, for whatever reason, she wanted to rule her own life. I know that it was not God that wanted to dominate her life. Satan was the one who wanted to dominate her life. He was not for her and never would be. God wanted a reciprocal relationship with her. I don't know how God could have been more generous. I know that this desire was not there when she was created because God looked at all He had created, and He said it was good. I wonder also at the knowledge the enemy had about the truthful part of this verse. When they ate of the tree, their eyes were opened and they were like God in the sense of knowing good and evil. How did Satan know that? I know she was blind as a bat as far as knowing evil as she was face to face with evil and did not realize it. I guess I need to go back to the fact that the devil is a liar and that if anyone continually hears a lie and accepts it, sooner or later they will believe it and live accordingly. I guess the next verse shows just how deceived she really was.

Genesis 3:6 And when the woman saw that the tree *was* good for food, and that it was pleasing to the eyes, and a tree to be desired to make wise, she took of its fruit, and ate. She also gave to her husband with her, and he ate.

Eve is looking at a tree that produces death! Because she did not believe what God said, it did not change what God said. It is hard to believe the comparisons, death, good for food, death, pleasing to the eye, death, desirable to gain wisdom. We don't know if Adam was there or if she went to get him, nor do we know what his view of the tree was, but we do know he also ate. I have often wondered what would have happened had Adam corrected Eve and not eaten. He could have went to God and told Him the situation, which God already obviously knew. I guess that is something we will never know. I suppose some would like to blame the woman, but the man ate also, fully aware he was not to do so. We also know that sin continued and progressed as Cain committed the first murder. God only knows how many murders have occurred since Cain. Sorry to say, sin is still increasing. We have sins today that, even though I know about them, are way beyond any desire I have to mention them and difficult to comprehend. Sin is still producing death, and not just the death brought about by murder, but death to so many areas of our lives, whether we are Christians or not. The death from sin is not discriminating; we select death when we eat of its fruit.

We have seen from scripture that the tree of death was not intended to cause death to Adam and Eve. The fruit of the tree of the knowledge of good and evil could not produce death unless the fruit was eaten. God did not design this tree for death, and He certainly did not say if you eat of this tree I will kill you. Let's be clear: the heart and motive of God was relationship. Choice was the issue. The bottom line in Eve's deception and wrong choice was that she believed the liar and paid the price and actually believed God to be the liar.

The enemy does not have any new tactics. He is still calling God a liar and defending sin as something good that will bless you. He still declares that you will surely not die. Does God actually hate sin? Yes, He does! The more important question is, why does God hate sin? Sin is defined in Greek as missing the mark. What mark are we missing when we sin? We are missing the same mark that Eve missed. We are believing the liar. There is no truth in him. The truth is, we still have the same choice that Eve had. God still wants a relationship with both sinners and saints. That has not changed, and that has been God's heart and motive all along.

John 3:16 For God so loved the world that He gave His only-begotten Son, that whoever believes in Him should not perish but have everlasting life. **17** For God did not send His Son into the world to condemn the world, but so that the world might be saved through Him.

If God loves all people but hates the sinner, how is it possible for Him to love and hate the same person? God does not hate the sinner; He loves the sinner. What He hates is sin and evil. Why? Because the sin is hurting and bringing death and separation to the sinner, who He loves and wants a relationship with, as well as to the saint, by stealing what He has for them. Jesus did not come to earth to condemn us but to deliver us.

Why not just get rid of the enemy and sin altogether, and there would be no temptation to sin? Once again, there can be no relationship without a choice. Remember, like the tree of the knowledge of good and evil, there was no death unless the fruit was eaten. So, sin is not the issue. The issue is not sinning.

Volition is not limited to salvation. We make choices all the time, and whether we like it or not, those choices have both good and bad consequences. The bad choices and their resulting consequences actually bring death into our lives. Thank God it is not our eternal life that dies, but sin does affect our lives while we are on this earth. Many saints give up years of their lives, as well as God's plans for them, through choices.

At this point, I hope to expose some of the major attacks of the enemy, but before doing so, I need to be very clear about something. If you are a Christian, you are in a war, and you are part of the army of God. When a person accepts Jesus as savior, he or she does so voluntarily. However, every saint is automatically drafted into God's army. Being in God's army is not a matter of choice or free will. Our battle is not against flesh and blood. It is against the kingdom of darkness and Satan, the prince of darkness. It is a strange battle as the overall war has already been won. Satan is already a defeated foe, and his days are numbered. However, as long as he has time, he will try to attack us through his lies and powerless threats. Also, in this warfare, the enemy cannot kill you. I don't want you to take my word for it, as we have God's Word that declares the truth. The following scriptures state both the opposing agendas of the enemy and Jesus, as well as Jesus' victory over the enemy. He destroyed Satan, who had the power of death.

John 10:10 The thief does not come except to steal and to kill and to destroy. I have come so that they might have life and that they might have *it* more abundantly.

Hebrews 2:14 Since then the children have partaken of flesh and blood, He also Himself likewise partook of the same; that through death He might destroy him who had the power of death (that is, the devil), **15** and deliver those who through fear of death were all their lifetime subject to bondage.

Colossians 2:15 Having stripped rulers and authorities, He made a show of them publicly, triumphing *over* them in it.

You can see from the verse from the gospel of John that the enemy's agenda is to steal, kill, and destroy. Our Lord's agenda is to give us life and life abundantly. These verses from the book of Hebrews declare that Satan, who had the power of death, no longer has that power. We do not have to fear death from the enemy. His only power is in his cunning lies, and we have God's word to expose all his lies and cunning maneuvers.

So what is sin anyway? We earlier discussed that it is basically missing the mark. So, if we are missing the mark, what mark are we missing? How do we know what the mark is? God has made it very clear in His Word what sin is and what missing the mark is. The dictionary defines sin as; an immoral act considered to be a transgression against divine law. One who commits sin violates or disobeys the will of God, as revealed in the Bible. From the book of first John, we have the following verse.

1 John 3:4 Everyone who practices sin also practices lawlessness, for sin is lawlessness.

So, just as in the garden, there was one law, and that law was to protect them from death. God has given us His laws to protect us from sin and death. We know that they did not trust God and ate of the tree that was restricted. We eat of the tree of the knowledge of good and evil every time we sin, and sin produces death when eaten. The truth is, what God is withholding from you is the death that will occur in your life if you eat of the tree. Through God's laws, He has directed us concerning what is good and what is to be avoided. Satan has taken God's laws and devised all manner of ways we can break them. When we break God's laws, which, remember, were given for our good, we eat of the tree, and we will experience death. No matter how much the enemy declares, we will certainly not die. Sin does produce death if eaten.

I gave the following illustration some serious consideration as to whether it was the area of sin that I wanted to use as an example of God's heart in the laws given and the enemy's lies concerning those laws. I don't intend to be crude in any way, but I will be truthful. One of the most shocking areas of sin in the entire world is sexual sin. I will not speak specifically to some areas as they are so gross, and they go way past the intent of what is being shared. First, let's be clear: God created man and woman. He created them to fit together and complete each other. The following verses state this.

Ephesians 5:31 "For this cause a man shall leave his father and mother and shall be joined to his wife, and the two of them shall be one flesh."

Mark 10:6 But from the beginning of the creation, God made them male and female.

God's creation of both male and female also includes their having sexual relations and the purposes for it. Without going into detail, it is pretty amazing how God created things in the man and the woman to fit together. He also actually created parts in both the man and the woman that would give pleasure, and He has no problem with sexual relations within marriage, He created it! The most amazing thing to me is how he created the woman and, through sexual relations, enabled her to become pregnant. Now, the couple could have one of the most amazing gifts that God could give us. My kids and grandkids are amazing gifts from God, and I thank Him for them. I can hardly believe that here in America, we are killing them by the millions. How twisted has the enemy made one of the most beautiful things on this earth, motherhood? Satan has twisted the gift and caused those gifted to be moms to actually become murderers. He did not create us like the animals either, where once in a while, we would go into heat and search for someone to mate with. It reminds me of people hanging out in the clubs, sniffing around for someone in heat. One of the difficult areas for men is guarding their eyes from checking out the bodies of the opposite sex. This is a temptation that doesn't leave; age does not make it go away. Something that greatly helped me with this area was a thought that I think came from an old chicken advertisement. Parts is parts! No matter what the packaging, behind all the fancy wrappings, parts is parts.

Homosexuals and lesbians who say that God created them the way they are need to understand that if this were true, he created them to become extinct as they cannot reproduce. If they want to have children, they have to adopt children created through God's plan, but at least they are not killing them. I know that God loves all sinners, and I am not trying to be mean or judgmental and I certainly do not hate them. Who knows what people have been through? God does! It was also God who gave them the ability to choose, even if the choice is deadly.

We need to understand and be very clear that God's laws are not against us, they are for us. They give us direction as to what to avoid and stay clear from. The enemy is constantly lying about God's heart and His laws. We can know the truth and confront and defeat His lies if we know what God's laws are. We can know His heart in giving them through our relationship with Him.

From here, I want to share a few areas where the enemy attacks Christians and exposes his lies.

One of the major attacks of the enemy is the security of our salvation. Within Christianity, we have two extremes concerning this issue. On one end of the spectrum, no sin can enter into heaven, and God hates sin, so we must be ever-vigilant in our choices and actions so that we do not lose our salvation. The question that is not answered is how much sin it takes to lose one's salvation. Is it one sin or the type of sin? What is not realized by many is that there is the sin of commission, where we actually commit the sin, but there is also the sin of omission, where we do not do what we are supposed to do. The truth is that, to some extent, we are all sinning, even if it is just having a bad attitude. No one is behaviorally perfect. Please don't misunderstand me, as I am not arguing for sin, and the Bible teaches that we are to continue to grow in our spiritual lives, which would clearly involve the reduction and removal of sin. This confusion concerning salvation causes many believers to live in fear all their lives. The other end of the spectrum would be those who believe in eternal salvation, that one can never lose their salvation no matter what they do or don't do. In both cases, we are looking for some level of sin that causes us to lose our salvation. I am not interested in debating or confusing the issue but merely pointing out the reality that many Christians fear losing their salvation and live in fear and insecurity. The truth is that we did nothing to deserve or earn salvation, Jesus paid for our sins. That leaves one wondering, if sin is death and Jesus gave His life to free us from it, why would we want to sin in the first place? Also, why ask for the same sin to be forgiven over and over? Why not pray for deliverance from the sin? The following scriptures, I hope, will give some encouragement.

Philippians 1:6 being confident of this very thing, that He who has begun a good work in you will perform *it* until the day of Jesus Christ,

John 10:27 My sheep hear My voice, and I know them, and they follow Me.

28 And I give to them eternal life, and they shall never ever perish, and not anyone shall pluck them out of My hand. **29** My Father who gave *them* to me is greater than all, and no one is able to pluck *them* out of My Father's hand. **30** I and the Father are one!

My sheep hear my voice. Therefore, if we are born again, we are His sheep, and we can truly hear His voice. We have His Word, and we know that He speaks to us through His Word; however, His Word does not answer everything. Major questions such as: Who should I marry? Where should I live? Where should I work, and so on and so forth are not spelled out in His Word. Where do we get the answers and directions? It is through our relationship with Him that we can hear His voice and get His directions for the individual questions that were mentioned. One vital choice for the believer is having a daily time with the Lord, building the relationship. We are to walk with him throughout the day as well, but without time spent together, the relationship is negatively affected. Time spent together is absolutely essential for a relationship. The enemy will do all manner of things to keep us from spending time with the Lord. Throughout the years of being a pastor, I have been amazed at how few Christians actually spend daily time with the Lord. Spending daily time with the Lord is Christianity 101. What was it that God wanted with us? Relationship!

Another major lie of the enemy is that sin separates us from God. It is true that if we are not born again, sin has separated us from God. Being born again removes our sin from us, and the door is then open for fellowship with God. After salvation, sin does not separate us from God. If it did, where would we go to get help in times of need and to receive forgiveness for sins? God is the source of forgiveness, and the following scripture clearly states that the opposite is true.

Hebrews 4:15 For we do not have a high priest who cannot be touched with the feelings of our infirmities, but was in all points tempted just as *we are, yet* without sin. **16** Therefore let us come boldly to the throne of grace, that we may obtain mercy and find grace to help in time of need.

That does not sound like we are separated from God, but rather, we are encouraged to come to His throne to get help. Jesus was tempted in all ways as we are tempted yet without sin. He knows and empathizes with our weaknesses. Many, because of feelings of guilt when they are tempted or when they sin, believe that God is mad at them. They, therefore, tend to run away from God rather than to Him. Once they have done penance of some sort, they believe they are now able to come to the throne. The latter action is worse than the former. We will never be able to approach the throne of God by our own efforts or righteousness. Our approach must be on the basis of Jesus paying for our sins. We are there to receive mercy and grace in our time of need. The tempter will tempt you to sin, and if you sin, he will condemn and lie to you, saying that God is upset and that you would be rejected if you approached him. If you do some sort of penance, then he will encourage you to go to the throne on your own merit, which will never be an accepted approach.

I am going to share with you a little bit about my life as a Christian. This is mine and my wife's jubilee year of salvation, as we have been saved now for fifty years. Over those years, I have learned a lot and still have a lot to learn. There were some sins that I struggled with for years. Not daily but from time to time. I would stand against the temptation, but in the end, I would give in and afterward would feel horrible and beg for God's forgiveness. I did not realize I could be delivered. I, too, ran from God and tried to do better, and when I felt like I was doing better, I then went to the throne, somewhat cowering but still wanting my relationship with the Father. As I grew in the Lord and spent more time with Him, I began to get free from some sins, but others hung on. I don't know how many times I struggled with temptation, only to give in and sin, and then take the path of self-chastisement and put forth a sincere effort at behavior modification. Time would pass, and I would eventually cower back to the Lord and ask for forgiveness. He graciously forgave me. One day, while spending time with the Lord, I had an awesome revelation that set me free from things that had tempted and troubled me for years. I read the following scripture, and my life changed.

2 Corinthians 5:17 So that if anyone *is* in Christ, *that one is* a new creature; old things have passed away; behold, all things have become new.

I realized that the old man had died, and I was a new creation with a new nature, and that I did not want to do what the devil was saying I did. He was playing on past sins and temptations from my memory bank. That is where the second part of this scripture came into play. Old things are passed away, and all things are made new. The next time the enemy came at me telling me what I wanted to do, I called him a liar. I said I am a new creation in Christ with a new nature, and it is not in my nature to want to do what you are suggesting. If he persisted in the battle, I did according to the following verses in Hebrews.

Hebrews 4:15 For we do not have a high priest who cannot be touched with the feelings of our infirmities, but was in all points tempted just as *we are, yet* without sin. **16** Therefore, let us come boldly to the throne of grace, that we may obtain mercy and find grace to help in time of need.

I would just go boldly to the throne of grace and cry out, "Help me, Jesus." I told him I choose against this sin, and I know that it is not in my heart to do so, as I am a new creation in you, and you have changed my very nature. Some of the most difficult battles have been gone for years now. I am not saying that I never sin or that I am perfect, but I am saying I know where to go for forgiveness and deliverance. I am also not the man I used to be, and I continue to change.

1 Corinthians 10:13 No temptation has taken you but *what is* common to man; but God *is* faithful, who will not allow you to be tempted above what you are able, but with the temptation also will make a way to escape, so that you may be able to bear *it.*

You do not have to eat of the fruit of the tree of the knowledge of good and evil. You can choose to trust God and follow Him here on earth and on into eternity.

Chapter 5: A Heart to Follow

Salvation is only the beginning. There are many who desire salvation simply to avoid hell. I can't blame them for not wanting to go to hell, but salvation is much more than fire insurance. I mentioned in a previous chapter that a simple prayer, followed with, "I'm good to go," is not the case at all. It is expected that salvation will be followed with a lifelong commitment of following the Lord. I think it should be very clear by now that being a Christian is about relationship and being a part of God's family, and that we must be born again. Surely if one is familiar with the Bible at all they would understand that God knows all things and is not bound by time. He can see before the beginning of time and after the ending of time. He knew you from before the beginning of time and had a plan for your life. Who could possibly choose a better plan for your life than God? Salvation involves a commitment to walk out that plan through a relationship with Him and obedience to His direction. I'm not saying that salvation is contingent on following that plan perfectly, but it is the expectation and should be our commitment. Jesus is not just our savior, He is to be our Lord, our supreme ruler and authority. I remember, as a new Christian facing the issue of His Lordship, with considerable trepidation. I thought that if I committed myself to him as my Lord, He would certainly call me as a missionary and send me across the world to some danger-filled jungle. I soon learned that He knows best and that His lordship was not as a dictator but as a loving Father who could be trusted with every decision. The following scriptures make it clear concerning the expectation.

Matthew 16:24 Then Jesus said to His disciples, If anyone desires to come after Me, let him deny himself and take up his cross and follow Me. **25** For whoever desires to save his life shall lose it, and whoever desires to lose his life for My sake shall find it. **26** For what is a man profited if he shall gain the whole world and lose his own soul? Or what shall a man give in exchange for his soul?

Even if we live to be a hundred years old, how can we compare that with eternity? Is it really such a great sacrifice to live for the Lord? The truth is, the real sacrifice is to not live for Him. Since, as children of the King, we are going to live forever, then even if we live to be a hundred years old, in relation to eternity, we are very young. For those who are not saved, the best life they will live here on earth is the best life they will ever live. The next life will be horrible. For those who are saved, the worst life they will live here on earth is the worst life they will ever live. Their next life will be awesome.

Even though being born again makes us a new creation, it is a spiritual rebirth and not a physical one. I said to the Lord, "I sure wish you had made my mind and body brand new as well." However, that change requires a transformation. The transformation process is not an overnight process but a lifelong process. The pace depends a lot on you, but the Lord can and will prompt you in certain areas where change is needed. Even after fifty years, I am still in the transformation process. I have asked the Lord to please not show me the list of changes yet to be made, but direct me to the next step. I am also very thankful for the changes made as I am not the person I was, but I am not yet the person I want to be. Our common goal, and God's will for our lives, is that we would be conformed to the image of Jesus, and with that comparison, I still have a long way to go. The following verses reveal the process.

Romans 12:1 I beseech you therefore, brothers, by the mercies of God to present your bodies a living sacrifice, holy, pleasing to God, *which is* your reasonable service. **2** And do not be conformed to this world, but be transformed by the renewing of your mind, in order to prove by you what *is* that good and pleasing and perfect will of God.

The apostle Paul uses the Greek word (parakaleō) for our English word beseech. In the Greek, the word has a variety of meanings. Basically, it is a call to come along side and includes an appeal extending even to the point of pleading and begging. The appeal is based on the mercies of God, which is his kindness in forgiving us and withholding our due punishment. He declares in light of the mercies of God that it is reasonable for us to present our bodies as a living sacrifice, holy and acceptable unto God. The justification that God has provided freely and the assurance of acceptance that we have as believers make this a reasonable request. It is a call to live a holy life and to follow the will and purposes of God individually. Jesus sacrificed His life for us, and we are to sacrifice our life for Him. This is the commitment required if we are to walk out the next part of this passage.

The second verse gives us the path of the transformation. We are first directed to not conform to this world, which means to not adapt ourselves, our minds, and our character to the world's pattern, nor follow the ways of the world. We are then instructed to be transformed, which means to change into another form, to transform, to modify. How is this to be accomplished? It is through the process of renewing our minds. Through this process, we can prove what is the good, acceptable, and perfect will of God.

Through our inherited sin, as well as our own sins, fellowship and relationship with God were not possible. Sin separated us from Him. Being born again, we have been made a new creation, and the connection to God was restored. Jesus paid for the sins that separated us from God, and we can now have open access to the Father. We also have the mind of Christ and His laws written on our hearts, as well as the ability to hear his voice. The scriptures state that His sheep hear His voice. It is through daily relationship with Him that we learn to hear His voice. This, too, is a process, and you can definitely know when He speaks to you and clearly understand what He is saying. I would like to insert a short testimony concerning hearing His voice. The first time I clearly heard His voice was years ago when I was a new Christian. I was in a coffee house street ministry, praying and telling the Lord that

I really wanted to hear His voice. I made a commitment that I would do what He said to do and say what He said to say. I did not hear an audible voice, but in my mind, it was very clear what He said to me. He said, "I want you to go over to that girl in the corner and tell her that I love her." I thought, "Yeah, right." I was disappointed as I really thought it was my own thoughts. He then said, "I thought you said you would say what I said to say and do what I said to do." I said, "You are right, I did." I got up and timidly approached her. I said, "I felt impressed to tell you that God loves you." She began to weep and told me that she was just praying and asking the Lord if He loved her. I was amazed and thought to myself, "What are the possibilities!"

When we are born again, we have the mind of Christ as we are now in relationship with the Father, and Jesus sent the Holy Spirit to dwell in us to be our guide and teacher. Our natural mind is carnal and the mind needs to be renewed. Scripture says that the carnal mind is enmity toward God. Enmity is defined as the state or feeling of being actively opposed or hostile to someone or something. This is the condition of the mind before conversion. It is the mind of the old man who died, and even though he is truly dead, we still have his thoughts and memories. Prior to salvation, our old man's thoughts and practices are what we were led by and lived by. Now, we can follow the leadership of the Holy Spirit. This is not always an easy path, as we will encounter resistance from the enemy. How you were raised can also, to some extent, define the difficulty of the battle. For instance, a young lady raised in a good home and taught the Word will not have the same battle ahead as a young lady who was molested by her father. Fortunately, they both have the same Lord who is able to heal all damages; however, the battle will not be the same. It is so easy to judge wrong statements or actions that do not line up with ours, but we do not have a clue what people have been through, and we are to pray for and help others, not judge them. We are not meant to fight alone, and the church should be more of a hospital than a court room. Ephesians 6:12 says, "For we wrestle not against flesh and blood, but against principalities, against powers, against the rulers of the darkness of this world, against spiritual wickedness in high places." We are all flesh and blood, and we are not enemies. As the accuser of the brethren, the enemy loves to separate and divide the body of Christ. Understanding the dynamics of the battle we are in is vitally important if you are to be win the fight. The following verses give us a summary.

Galatians 5:14 For all the Law is fulfilled in one word, *even* in this, "You shall love your neighbor as yourself." **15** But if you bite and devour one another, take heed that you are not consumed by one another. **16** I say, then, Walk in *the* Spirit, and you shall not fulfill *the* lusts of *the* flesh. **17** For the flesh lusts against the Spirit, and the Spirit against the flesh. And these are contrary to one another; lest whatever you may will, these things you do.

The flesh refers to mere human nature, the earthly nature of man apart from divine influence, and therefore prone to sin and opposed to God. Our minds and our bodies were not created new when we were born again. We are spirit beings living in a body, and our spirit was created new, but not our mind or our bodies. Our minds are to be renewed according to the mind of Christ, the Word of God, and the direction of the Holy Spirit who dwells in our spirit. The body will follow the dictates of the mind, so the flesh, which is prone to sin, can be controlled by us through the renewing of the mind. The enemy works through our minds and through are bodily appetites to draw us into sin. There is a warfare going on between the Spirit and the flesh. If one wills to do good, he is opposed by the enemy through the flesh, and if to do evil, he is opposed by the Spirit. The following portion of scripture has to do with the battle just described.

Romans 8:5 For they who are according to the flesh mind the things of flesh, but they who are according to the Spirit the things of the Spirit. **6** For to be carnally minded *is* death, but to be spiritually minded *is* life and peace **7** because the carnal mind *is* enmity against God, for it is not subject to the Law of God, neither indeed can *it be*. **8** So then they who are in the flesh cannot please God. **9** But you are not in the flesh, but in *the* Spirit, if *the* Spirit of God dwells in you. But if anyone has not *the* Spirit of Christ, he is none of His. **10** And if Christ *is* in you, indeed the body *is* dead because of sin, but the Spirit *is* life because of righteousness. **11** But if the Spirit of the *One* who raised up Jesus from *the* dead dwells in you, the *One* who raised up Christ from *the* dead shall also make your mortal bodies alive by His Spirit who dwells in you. **12** Therefore, brothers, we are not debtors to the flesh, to live according to the flesh.

13 For if you live according to the flesh, you shall die. But if you through *the* Spirit mortify the deeds of the body, you shall live. **14** For as many as are led by *the* Spirit of God, they are the sons of God

From the beginning of time on earth, the issue that destroyed the life God intended for His creation was sin. No matter how much the enemy tries to convince us that we will surely not die, it is an absolute lie. Sin has, from the beginning, produced death, and it will do so until it is completely done away with in heaven, our new paradise. Until then, we can indeed overcome sin and not experience the death that sin produces. Remember that the tree of the knowledge of good and evil did not produce death. It could not harm Adam and Eve, and the only way death could come to them was if they ate of it. It is the same today. Death will not come to us if we do not eat of the fruit and suffer death. It is vitally important that we understand that death has been defeated and God has broken the power of sin. The scriptures below declare that truth:

Romans 6:1 What shall we say then? Shall we continue in sin so that grace may abound? **2** Let it not be! How shall we who died to sin live any longer in it? **3** Do you not know that as many of us as were baptized into Jesus Christ were baptized into His death? **4** Therefore we were buried with Him by baptism into death, so that as Christ was raised up from *the* dead by the glory of the Father; even so we also should walk in newness of life. **5** For if we have been joined together in the likeness of His death, we shall also be *in the likeness* of His resurrection; **6** knowing this, that our old man is crucified with *Him* in order that the body of sin might be destroyed, that from now on we should not serve sin. **7** For he who died has been justified from sin. **8** But if we died with Christ, we believe that we shall also live with Him, **9** knowing that when Christ was raised from *the* dead, He dies no more; death no longer has dominion over Him. **10** For in that He died, He died to sin once; but in that He lives, He lives to God. **11** Likewise count yourselves also to be truly dead to sin, but alive to God through Jesus Christ our Lord. **12** Therefore do not let sin reign in your mortal body, that you should obey it in its lusts. **13** Do not yield your members *as* instruments of unrighteousness to sin, but yield yourselves to God, as *one* alive from *the* dead, and your members *as* instruments of righteousness to God.

Reckon yourselves dead to sin. Recon means to consider, take into account, weigh, and meditate on. At the end of the last chapter, I explained how I had realized that I was a new creation and that it was not in my nature to sin. In fact, it was against my nature to sin. So when the enemy would bring an accusation or a temptation, I would declare him to be a liar and stand on the reality that it was not me who wanted to do what he was saying I wanted to do. The old man is truly dead, and we are a new creation. We are also under God's grace, which is His unmerited favor, and not under the law. We are not judged by the law any longer. Jesus died for all our sins and broke sin's power over us. Verse 11 above states clearly that we are to reckon ourselves dead to sin, but alive to God.

Thankfully, even if we slip up and do sin, there is forgiveness. However, forgiveness was never intended for continual willful sins. We must remember that the desire to sin is no longer ours if we are born again. It is not in our nature and actually is against our nature. I have said it before, but I will say it again: why continue to ask forgiveness for sin over and over again? Why not ask for deliverance and learn to resist the external desire to sin? I say external because it is from the evil one, through the flesh, that the temptations come and not from the Spirit or from us. The following scripture from the book of James explains the process of temptation and sin.

James 1:13 Let no one being tempted say, I am tempted from God. For God is not tempted by evils, and He tempts no one. **14** But each one is tempted by his lusts, being drawn away and seduced *by them*. **15** Then when lust has conceived, *it* brings forth sin. And sin, when it is fully formed, brings forth death.

James is speaking specifically about temptation to sin, which God will never bring to us. We may have trials that God allows to help us grow or train us in some specific area, but God will never tempt us to sin. James is making a specific clarification here between trials and temptations. We are tempted when we are dragged away by our own evil desire, and when the desire is conceived, it gives birth to sin, and sin always leads to death. Why would God give us desires that open us up for temptation? Why would He give us sexual desires that open Pandora's box to all sorts of sin? He did so, as we have discussed in another chapter, that we might have children and that we might, within the bonds of marriage and only there, procreate and enjoy the process. It is the enemy that takes advantage of those desires and produces all manner of ways whereby we can supposedly fulfill them outside of God's parameters. When the natural desire is given a means to fulfill that desire outside of what God gave it for, and we take that path, we enter into sin. Not only that, but we will find out that nothing outside of God's plan will fulfill those desires. Sin only leaves you wanting more as it never fulfills. The enemy is a clever negotiator, and if he sees an opening, he will take it. One of his ploys is to compare sins and categorize them as little sins or big sins. He will say,

"Well, even if you are sinning, this sin is not as bad as that sin. You can check out some porno as you are not committing adultery. After all, you are not hurting anyone, and you do have needs." The sad thing is that you are committing adultery. In fact, the scripture takes an even stronger view of adultery, as you can see from the words of Jesus in the following verse from Matthew.

Matthew 5:28 But I say to you that whoever looks on a woman to lust after her has already committed adultery with her in his heart.

We are to repent of our sins. This does not mean saying we are sorry and asking for forgiveness. We need more than being sorry and asking forgiveness, we need to stop sinning. Repentance is so many times used as forgiveness, when repentance means a change of mind and a complete 180-degree turn around, heading in the opposite direction. We are to turn from sin unto righteousness, and we can do so by the power of God. He will enable us to be free from sin and not have to ask for forgiveness over and over again.

It is a strange warfare as the battle is really in the mind. It is where he attacks us with his lies, accusations, temptations, and condemnation. We have to guard our thought life. It is not just some thoughts, but every thought. Take a look at the following verses.

2 Corinthians 10:4 For the weapons of our warfare *are* not fleshly, but mighty through God to the pulling down of strongholds, **5** pulling down imaginations and every high thing that exalts itself against the knowledge of God, and bringing into captivity every thought into the obedience of Christ;

Philippians 4:8 Finally, my brothers, whatever things are true, whatever things *are* honest, whatever *things are* right, whatever *things are* pure, whatever *things are* lovely, whatever *things are* of good report; if *there is* any virtue and if *there is* any praise, think on these things.

The word exhorts us to live a holy life, and therefore, by His power and His grace, we can.

Chapter 6: FORGIVE?

Satan is the accuser of the brethren, and he is relentless in his accusations. He not only accuses us to each other, but he also accuses us to God and God to us. The enemy accuses God to us in an attempt to diminish our trust in God. His goal in the body of Christ is to divide and conquer. I mentioned in the last chapter that we are to stand together and that we do not fight alone; however, if we can be lured into fighting with each other, then the enemy has gained a significant victory. Unforgiveness is a cancer that affects us both spiritually and physically. It can literally eat us alive. It is not only deadly to us individually, but it can also be deadly to others. The enemy's accusations do not have to be based on lies. At times, they are actually based on the truth. I don't think that there is any of us who have not experienced offenses and damages from our past. However, not all offenses are actually offenses, as they can be assumed offenses. Just because someone takes offense at something said or some action taken does not necessarily mean that what was said or done was truly offensive. We live in a world where if you simply do not agree with someone, it is taken as an offense. Sadly, whether the offense is real or assumed, the damage can be the same, especially if it leads to unforgiveness.

Over the years of counseling, I have seen the results of unforgiveness in the lives of my clients as well as in my own life. I have observed the following process over and over, caused by offense and unforgiveness. A true offense or an assumed offense will lead to the same steps. Unforgiveness begins with offense and leads to blame or accusation. If we do not forgive, blame will lead to anger. If we continue in our unforgiveness, anger will lead to bitterness, and bitterness can spread to others. The following verses declare that not only will you be defiled, but that many will be defiled.

Hebrews 12:14 Follow peace with all, and holiness, without which no one shall see the Lord; **15** looking diligently lest any fail of the grace of God, or lest any root of bitterness springing up disturb *you*, and by it many are defiled,

Bitterness will lead to hatred, and the final step with unforgiveness is murder. That does not mean that you actually kill the person, but it could happen. Often the relationship is seriously damaged or completely destroyed, and although the person is alive, they are dead to you. Forgiveness is the only cure and will work at any level, from blame to murder. It has been said that unforgiveness is like drinking poison that you intended for the offender. I know of cases where the one being blamed doesn't even know there has been an offense. At times it is just a misunderstanding. Whatever the case, unforgiveness is a serious issue.

We learned from Genesis that blaming was an immediate result of the fall. When confronted by God, Adam blamed Eve, saying it was the woman you gave me, insinuating that it was God who was really at fault. Eve blamed the devil, saying the serpent beguiled me. They did not seek forgiveness and restoration because, after all, they were not at fault. Not taking responsibility for their actions was a clear sign of the fallen nature, and they were manifesting the characteristics of their father, the accuser. Blame ignites the whole process defined above. It is our responsibility to go to the person and hopefully try and work things out before things get out of hand. The biblical view is that both parties are to try and work things out. If we have something against someone, we are to go to them, and if they have something against us, we are to go to them. The same course of action is a biblical command for them as well.

To assist in understanding the process and damages of unforgiveness, I decided to share a testimony from my own life. I was pastoring and was in prayer one morning when the Lord said to me that He wanted me to forgive my dad. I laughed. I replied, "I have forgiven him a hundred times," I laughed again and said, "well, you got me." "Obviously, if I had forgiven him a hundred times, I had not really forgiven him." My next response was, "okay, why have I not been successful?" I did not like His answer. He told me that I had to forget. I said, "no way, he doesn't deserve it!" For three weeks I resisted His direction. I was determined I was not going to forget. I finally relented and said, "I know that you know best, and if that is what I must do to truly forgive, then that is what I will do."

It is irrelevant what I was blaming him for, and thankfully I do not remember much of it anyway. I also do not know how much of what I was blaming him for was even true. Unforgiveness clouds your perspective, and when you are angry and hateful toward someone, they can do nothing right. One thing I did learn right away was that I was a lot like him. I realized that my negative focus on my dad was actually creating in me some of the same issues. I knew that memorization requires rehearsing, and to forget requires refusing to rehearse. It took some time, and I was amazed that I began to change. What was even more surprising was that I began to remember the good things about my dad. I could not see any good while trapped in the hellhole of unforgiveness. I had been chained to my unforgiveness, and it was damaging me. God knew I wanted to forgive and that I had really tried to do the right thing; however, the enemy was there to remind me of the offenses, and whether actual or assumed, they did the job. I am so thankful to the Lord for delivering me from my unforgiveness, and before my dad passed, God graciously gave me an opening to heal the relationship. Things were good between us, and I was honored to do his funeral.

Even from the grave, the people you have blamed and have not forgiven can affect your life. Unforgiveness can affect our choices and attitudes and can easily be used by the enemy. Truthfully, it is giving some control in our lives to the person we have not forgiven. Why should someone else control our emotions? Since they are to blame, we have to change them to be free. If they are the problem, then they must change. After all, it is their fault. We find ourselves avoiding them and hurts can lead to gossip, and the cancer can spread to others. Sometimes it is difficult, if not impossible, to avoid them, so avoidance doesn't always help. What if it is a family member or a mate? I once had a client, who obviously will remain unnamed, who gave me the amount of years, months, days, and hours it had been since her husband had offended her. I just about fell out of my seat. She forgave him, and her life changed drastically. I know that with my dad, the blame and unforgiveness were used as an excuse for my own failures. If this and that had not happened, I would be different and be successful. After all, if it is his fault, I can't change it. I have to get him to confess that he is wrong and heal this. What if I was offended by ten different people? Now I would have to change ten people in order to be free. Forgiveness is not for the other person, it is for you. You can't control their life, but you can control your own. You have to take responsibility for your own life.

The following verses clearly define the seriousness of forgiveness. It is a verse that has caused considerable anxiety for many believers.

Matthew 6:14 For if you forgive men their trespasses, your heavenly Father will also forgive you; **15** but if you do not forgive men their trespasses, neither will your Father forgive your trespasses.

This portion of scripture follows the Lord's response to the disciples when they asked if He would teach them how to pray. In that prayer, we, as His disciples, are instructed to pray that God would forgive our debts as we forgive our debtors. It is clear from the Lord's Prayer that if we want forgiveness, it is contingent on our forgiving others. If not taken within the context of all scripture, it would appear that I would have been unforgiven for a number of years while sincerely trying to forgive my dad. I know that this was not the case. I also know that God knows our hearts. It was not in my heart to hold unforgiveness, as I sincerely tried to forgive. Is unforgiveness an unforgivable sin? Had I totally rejected the Lord's counsel, would I have lost my salvation? Doesn't the Lord discipline those He loves rather than cast them out? Granted, if I refuse to forgive someone, whether a real offense or not, then I should not think that I would receive forgiveness. I guess if I thought that I deserved forgiveness while assuming that others whom I had aught against did not deserve it, I could mistakenly justify my unforgiveness. The truth is we do not deserve forgiveness, so it is not a basis for withholding forgiveness. God was patient with me and got me to the point where I did forgive. He was also aware of the hurt and damages that were done. Not all that I was angry and unforgiving about was untrue. Wrong things did happen. I think it was those things, as well as some of the assumed issues, that caused my determination to not forgive. I am so thankful for His patience and understanding, but most of all for His deliverance. God has also promised that He would never leave me nor forsake me, that no one could take me out of the Father's hand. He promises in His word to finish the work in our lives that He started. He is faithful even when we are not. He is dedicated to delivering us from all sin, and by faith, we can walk in the assurance that we will be with Him in glory one day.

We know that God does forgive, but how does God forgive? The following scriptures tell us.

Psalms 103:10 He has not dealt with us according to our sins, nor rewarded us according to our iniquities. **11** For as the heavens *are* high above the earth, *so* is His mercy toward those who fear Him. **12** As far as the east *is* from the west, *so* far has He removed our transgressions from us.

Hebrews 10:17 also, *He adds*, "their sins and their iniquities I will remember no more."

In Greek, the word for no more is (ou me) and means never, certainly not, not at all, by no means. So when the Lord forgives our sins, He forgets them and will remember them no more.

Should we expect that it is different for us? If we are to truly forgive, we must forget.

In the following portion of scripture, we can see that it is vitally important that we not excuse our unforgiveness, even if the person we are forgiving offends us over and over again. Our forgiveness cannot be excused, even if others repeat the offense. Our forgiveness must be in obedience to the Lord. The apostle Peter wonders about forgiveness as well, and in the following discourse, we have his questions and the Lord's answer.

Matthew 18:21 Then Peter came to Him and said, Lord, how often shall my brother sin against me and I forgive him? Until seven times? **22** Jesus said to him, I do not say to you, Until seven times; but, Until seventy times seven. **23** Therefore the kingdom of Heaven has been compared to a certain king who desired to make an accounting with his servants. **24** And when he had begun to count, one was brought to him who owed him ten thousand talents.

Even if you could forgive seventy times seven, which would be 490 times, it would not mean that on the 491st time, you would not have to forgive. I would think that seven times would be difficult, and the point of the Lord's answer was to keep on forgiving. To repent means the offender would have changed his or her mind and asked for forgiveness. I think we can safely say, with complete assurance, that forgiveness is to be continuous.

What about trust? How am I to trust a person who would do things against me over and over, which is the case in the last portion of scripture? Even if they came back over and over again and repented they were to be forgiven, but what about trust? Trust is certainly a factor in relationships, as we saw from the very beginning of time. Volition and the tree of the knowledge of good and evil were for the purpose of seeing if Adam and Eve would choose to trust God. Are we to blindly trust, no matter what? What if the offense was against one of our children? What if the offender was a pedophile? If trust is truly a factor in relationships, then how could I possibly have a relationship with a person who would offend me over and over again? How could I possibly forgive a pedophile for abusing my child, let alone trust them? I know it would take the grace of God to forgive in this circumstance, but I certainly would not trust him with my child. We are to turn the other cheek, which means to remain open, but it does not mean that we are never to resist evil or simply allow ourselves to be beaten to death. I think that Romans 13 probably deals with this issue the best, as forgiveness is one thing but justice is another. I think that the following portion of Romans would include the police as those who enforce the law.

Romans 13:3 For the rulers are not a terror to good works, but to the bad. And do you desire to be not afraid of the authority? Do the good, and you shall have praise from it. **4** For it is a servant of God to you for good. For if you practice evil, be afraid, for it does not bear the sword in vain; for it is a servant of God, a revenger for wrath on him who does evil.

 I know that with the authorities, trust is not a factor with criminal offenses, and although the offenders could be forgiven, in jail, they are not free to continue their damaging behavior. I would hope and pray that they would find the Lord and be forgiven, as I do not wish anyone to go to hell. Not to belabor the issue, but what about infidelity? This certainly affects the trust issue. Even within the scriptures, this sin is certainly to be forgiven, but the trust issue is damaged, and divorce is allowed. I will leave the trust issue at this point.

I think that when we are offended, most of us would like to retaliate. It doesn't seem fair that the offender should get away with it. Jesus said that offenses must come, but woe to the one offending. Although it is not something that we are to rejoice over, the Bible states that you will reap what you sow. Throughout the Bible, *sowing* is used as a metaphor for one's actions and *reaping* for the results of those actions. The Bible does not say that this will occur immediately, nor does it give any timelines for the reaping. The following scripture also makes it very evident that we will reap what we sow.

Galatians 6:7 Do not be deceived, God is not mocked. For whatever a man sows, that he also will reap.

We are to trust the Lord that He will deal with the issues and offenses. We are further instructed not to take vengeance. In Romans 12:18-19 we see why we do not have to take vengeance. We have the word of the Lord that He will repay

Romans 12:18 If it be possible, as much as lies in you, live peaceably with all men. **19** Dearly beloved, avenge not yourselves, but rather give place unto wrath: for it is written, Vengeance is mine; I will repay, saith the Lord.

We already know that we are to forgive and not take revenge. Surprisingly, we are instructed to do the very opposite.

Romans 12:20 Therefore if your enemy hungers, feed him. If he thirsts, give him drink. For *in so* doing you shall heap coals of fire on his head. **21** Do not be overcome by evil, but overcome evil with good.

Overcome evil with good. The scriptures also say that when you do good to those who offend and misuse you, you heap hot coals on their head. I don't think that should be the goal, but it is good to realize that it may convict them of their bad behavior and turn things around.

I will finish this chapter with what I believe is one of the hardest areas to forgive: yourself. The same effects will be present if you do not forgive yourself. If you blame yourself, you will be angry with yourself, and if this continues, you will be bitter with yourself, and then hatred will set in and finally murder. God knows your every wrong thought, motive, and sin. Nothing is hidden from Him, and yet if you are born again, He has forgiven you and remembers those things no more. If past failures and sins plague you, then either it is from you who has not forgiven yourself or from the enemy pouring salt in the wounds. The same admonition is relevant to you! You must forgive yourself, or you won't be forgiven. God will not remind you of the things He has forgiven and remembers no more. Self-hatred can lead to suicide. When we remember the failures and sins of the past, we need to stand against those thoughts and realize that they are from the enemy and not from God. Take the admonition and do good for yourself. After all, you are to bless those who misuse you, so stop misusing yourself and be blessed.

Chapter 7: Faith

The words faith and believe represent another area of misunderstanding. I think this is due mainly to its broad usage in everyday conversation; however, the numerous ways these words are used are quite different from their biblical meaning. The dictionary definition for faith is complete trust or confidence in someone or something. So, what does faith mean according to the Bible? The closest that the Bible comes to offering an exact definition is in Hebrews 11:1: Now faith is the assurance of things hoped for, the conviction of things not seen. The central biblical theme for faith is confidence or trust, and the object of faith is God and His word.

Obviously, there are people who do not believe that there is a God. An agnostic is a person who believes that nothing is known or can be known of the existence or nature of God or of anything beyond material phenomena and who claims neither faith nor disbelief in God. An atheist is a person who disbelieves in the existence of God or gods. Others say that they believe there is a God, but their belief is only in His existence, and sadly they do not know Him. Believing that God exists and that you are therefore saved aligns with believing that you can achieve salvation through religious practices, which is the purpose of my writing this book. Many people believe in God, that is in God's existence, and claim to be Christians but do not know Him. Religious observances, as a means of salvation, is a lie. Simply believing that God exists and that you therefore are saved is also a lie. Simply believing that God exists does not result in salvation and is not biblical faith.

In the book of James, there is a discussion of works and faith and that faith without works is dead. However, this is not works as a means of salvation, but the reality that salvation is supposed to produce good works. These good works are ordained by God, that we should walk in them. They are not the means to salvation.

Good works are the outcome of being born again. The following verses state this.

Ephesians 2:8 For by grace you are saved through faith, and that not of yourselves, *it is* the gift of God, **9** not of works, lest anyone should boast.

The scripture declares that we are saved by grace and it is through faith. Salvation is a gift received by faith. It is also evident that works are an expected part of salvation and that God ordained that we should walk in them. We are to live a life of obedience to God. As stated in the other chapters of this book, it is all about relationship. Merely believing that He exists is not the same. Those who believe that they are saved because they proclaim that they believe that God exists or that they perform religious rituals have believed a lie. To simply believe something to be true is not biblical faith and it does not make it true. The Bible says that the demons believe, and yet they are not saved, but their belief is real enough to cause them to tremble with fear. It would seem that since they believe, that they have faith. They know that He exists and they fear Him, but they certainly are not saved, nor does their belief in His existence save them. They also do not have any works that are a part of salvation. In fact, the opposite is true; their works are against God. They absolutely do not have a trust and reliance on God. They do believe, but they do not have faith. It obviously takes more than belief that God exists to have faith and be saved. The enemy has designed the lie that belief in God's existence is enough. The word belief in the scriptures has basically the same meaning as faith. However, true faith and belief are more than mere recognition of God's existence. The enemy has substituted the acknowledgment of God's existence as faith. You may truly believe in God's existence and still not have biblical faith. The scriptures are clear that you are either for Him or against Him. You may not realize it, but if you are not born again, you are against Him. Granted, it may be due to being born with a fallen nature and separated from God, but you are still against Him. However, the remedy for our fallen nature and separation from God has been provided by Jesus' death on the cross. There is only one name by which one may be saved. Faith does not earn it receives. We cannot earn our salvation, but by faith, we receive what Jesus has done for us and accept the free gift of salvation.

Faith is a receiver and not a provider. The redemptive work of Jesus is completed, and all that is needed for a life of holiness and victory has been provided. By faith in God's grace, His unmerited favor and provision, we can receive what God has provided, but we can never work for or earn anything from God by faith. Our faith will never produce for us, but it can receive all that is needed through the gracious provision of our Father. Faith is the means by which we receive our salvation as well as all other provisions.

Faith is much more than an intellectual agreement of God's existence. I took the following illustrations from my studies on faith, as they demonstrate the difference between simply believing and true faith.

Imagine you are at Niagara Falls watching a tightrope walker push a wheelbarrow across a rope high above the falls. After watching him go back and forth several times, he asks for a volunteer to sit in the wheelbarrow as he pushes it across the falls. At an intellectual level, you may believe that he could successfully push you across the rope over the falls, but you are not exercising biblical faith until you get in the wheelbarrow and entrust yourself to the tightrope walker. True faith requires action.

Every person on the face of the earth has faith and in fact, lives by faith in some area and to some degree. One example is our trust in traffic lights. We believe that if a traffic light is green, the other lane has a red light and that we can safely proceed. We believe that the light is functioning properly and place our lives in the hands of technology. We also believe that other drivers will obey the red light and stop. We do not close our eyes and hope but have put our faith in the proper functioning of the light and the obedience of other drivers. Our faith is seen in the action we take in going through the green light and stopping at the red light. I have not had a traffic light fail yet, but they could malfunction and fail. God never fails, and His promises are true and absolutely trustworthy.

True faith shows itself through our actions. We are to commit our lives to God and follow Him. The word says that he who chooses to save his life will lose it, but he who loses his life for My sake will find it. These are the words of Jesus. Why wouldn't we give our lives for Him since He gave His life for us? Even if we could live a thousand years on this earth, what is that compared to eternity with God? The commitment is much more than a mere declaration that you believe that God exists. If we claim to have faith, then it must be manifested in our actions. In a letter to the Jewish believers, Jesus' disciple James reminds them of this fact.

James 2:17 Even so, if it does not have works, faith is dead, being by itself. **18** But someone will say, You have faith, and I have works. Show me your faith without your works, and I will show you my faith from my works. **19** You believe that there is one God, you do well; even the demons believe and tremble. **20** But will you know, O vain man, that faith without works is dead? **21** Was not Abraham our father justified by works when he had offered Isaac his son upon the altar? **22** Do you see how faith worked with his works, and from the works faith was made complete?

Verse 21 speaks of Abraham, who was the father of faith and is a prime example of true biblical faith. You can read about his life in the book of Genesis. I will relate some of his story in my own words. I hope to bring out, not only his example of faith, but two other aspects of faith, the testing of faith and the growth of faith.

We do not know why God chose Abraham. Abraham was a sinful heathen who grew up in an unbelieving and idolatrous society. We do not know exactly how or when God first made Himself known to Abraham, but Abraham was raised in a home that was pagan and served other gods, so he was not chosen because of his righteousness. He may have had higher moral standards than his friends and neighbors, but this was not the reason God chose him. God chose him because He wanted to choose him, and when God spoke to him, he listened; when God promised, he trusted; when God commanded, he obeyed.

Joshua 24:2 And Joshua said to all the people, So says Jehovah, the God of Israel, Your fathers lived Beyond the River in times past, Terah the father of Abraham, and the father of Nahor, and they served other gods.

Abraham was a descendant of Noah's son Shem. His native city was in Ur of Chaldea, located in the general area of Mesopotamia, between the Tigris and the Euphrates rivers, near where the Garden of Eden was located. It was not Abraham's plan to leave Ur or Haran and settle in the land of Canaan; it was God's plan. He heard the call of God and obeyed immediately. When he left Haran, he had no idea where he was going. He was called by God, and only God knew where he was going. The following scriptures portray the beginning of Abraham's walk of faith and His calling.

Genesis 12:1 And Jehovah said to Abram, Go out of your country, and from your kindred, and from your father's house into a land that I will show you. **2** And I will make you a great nation. And I will bless you and make your name great. And you shall be a blessing. **3** And I will bless those that bless you and curse the one who curses you. And in you shall all families of the earth be blessed. **4** And Abram departed, even as Jehovah had spoken to him. And Lot went with him. And Abram was seventy-five years old when he departed from Haran. **5** And Abram took Sarai his wife, and Lot his brother's son, and all their substance that they had gathered, and the souls that they had gained in Haran. And they went forth to go into the land of Canaan. And they came into the land of Canaan.

The scriptures do not say that Abraham was disobedient in taking his father, even though it says from your father's house. The reality is that when they ventured out, they stopped at Haran and settled there. Why they stopped there is not clear. After Abraham's father died, the Lord spoke to him again and told him to leave Haran and go into the land He had promised him.

Hebrews 11:8 By faith Abraham obeyed when he was called to go out into a place which he was afterward going to receive for an inheritance. And *he* went out, not knowing where he went. **9** By faith he lived in the land of promise as a stranger, dwelling in tents with Isaac and Jacob, the heirs of the same promise with him.

Abraham made some mistakes on his journey of faith, but he learned to trust God more with every mistake. He grew into a man of unwavering faith. Like Abraham, no one comes to God as a righteous person, and we will also make mistakes in our walk of faith. Like Abraham, we will not know all that God has planned for us or allows in our life, but we can learn to trust Him and walk in obedience. If you are a born-again believer, you are a descendant of Abraham, and like Abraham, you will also find that God is faithful and trustworthy. In the following account, we find that Abraham actually lied and deceived the Pharaoh of Egypt.

The scriptures do not say that Abraham was directed by God to go into Egypt; however, there was a famine in the land, which was the reason for his going into Egypt. The events of this trip into Egypt were not a manifestation of Abraham's faith. In fact, they were a manifestation of his lack of faith, both in God's protection and in God's ability and faithfulness to provide within the promised land. His lying to Pharaoh is further evidence that Abraham was not chosen because of his righteousness. The following account details Abraham's trip to Egypt.

Hebrews 12:10 For truly they chastened *us* for a few days according to their own pleasure, but He for our profit, that *we* might be partakers of His holiness. **11** Now chastening for the present does not seem to be joyous, but grievous; nevertheless afterward it yields the peaceable fruit of righteousness to those who are exercised by it. **12** Because of this, straighten up the hands which hang down and the enfeebled knees. **13** And make straight paths for your feet, lest that which is lame be turned out of the way, but let it rather be healed. **14** Follow peace with all, and holiness, without which no one shall see the Lord; **15** looking diligently lest any fail of the grace of God, or lest any root of bitterness springing up disturb *you*, and by it many are defiled, **16** (lest there *be* any fornicator, or profane person like Esau, who for one morsel of food sold his birthright. **17** For you know that afterward, when he desired to inherit the blessing, he was rejected; for he did not find any place of repentance, though he sought it carefully with tears). **18** For you have not come to the mountain that might be touched and that burned with fire, nor to blackness and darkness and tempest, **19** and the sound of a trumpet, and the voice of words (which *voice* they who heard begged that a word should not be spoken to them anymore, **20** for they could not endure the thing commanded, "And if so much as a beast should touch the mountain, it shall be stoned or thrust through with a dart,"

It is obvious from this account that Abraham's motive for lying was not to deceive them for some evil purpose but to save his life. However, he did believe that lying would save his life. He was certainly not directed by God to lie. Sarah was obedient to her husband and agreed to say that she was his sister. So Abraham's trust in a lie caused his wife to follow the same path and lie. Strangely, it is evident that Abraham was right about her physical appearance and that she would be viewed as beautiful, and that someone might, if they believed that she was his wife, kill him to have her as a wife for themselves. It was fortunate that she ended up in Pharaoh's house, as it is apparent that he was not a man who would kill Abraham to take Sarah as his wife. Even though Abraham lied for fear of losing his life, God still intervened for him. We do not know what the plagues were, but they are identified as great. Also, we do not know how Pharaoh discovered that Sarah was Abraham's wife. Perhaps she told him. It is not clear whether Pharaoh attributed the plagues to God or why he would have questioned Sarah. Whatever the case, God did not put plagues on Abraham for lying but instead protected him. Also, he kept Pharaoh from marrying Sarah. I suppose Pharaoh could have killed Abraham and taken Sarah for his wife; after all, he was Pharaoh, and who would stop him? The reality that he could have married her apparently caused a considerable amount of consternation for Pharaoh. Abraham is sent from the land with all the possessions that Pharaoh had given him because of Sarah.

A clear example of Abraham's faith and trust in God is his encounter with God in Genesis 15.

Genesis 15:1 After these things the Word of Jehovah came to Abram in a vision, saying, Fear not, Abram, I *am* your shield and your exceeding great reward. **2** And Abram said, Lord God, what will You give me, since I *am* going childless, and the steward of my house *is* this Eliezer of Damascus? **3** And Abram said, Behold, You have given no seed to me. And behold, one born in my house is my heir. **4** And behold, the Word of Jehovah *came* to him saying, This one shall not be your heir. But he that shall come forth out of your own bowels shall be your heir. **5** And He brought him outside and said, Look now toward the heavens and count the stars, if you are able to count them. And He said to him, So shall your seed be. **6** And he believed in Jehovah. And He counted it to him for righteousness.

Genesis 16:1 Now Sarai, Abram's wife, did not bear. And she had a female slave, an Egyptian, and her name *was* Hagar. **2** And Sarai said to Abram, Behold now, Jehovah has kept me from bearing. I pray you, go in to my slave woman. It may be that I may be built by her. And Abram listened to the voice of Sarai. **3** And Sarai, Abram's wife, took Hagar her slave woman, the Egyptian, and gave her to her husband Abram to be his wife (after Abram had lived ten years in the land of Canaan). **4** And he went in to Hagar, and she conceived. And when she saw that she had conceived, her mistress was despised in her eyes. **5** And Sarai said to Abram, My wrong *be* upon you. I have given my slave woman into your bosom, and when she saw that she had conceived, I was despised in her eyes. Jehovah judge between me and you. **6** But Abram said to Sarai, Behold, your slave woman *is* in your hand. Do to her as it pleases you. And Sarai dealt harshly with her, and she fled from her face. **7** And the Angel of Jehovah found her by a fountain of water in the wilderness, by the fountain in the way to Shur. **8** And He said, Hagar, Sarai's slave, where did you come from? And where will you go? And she said, I flee from the face of my mistress Sarai. **9** And the Angel of Jehovah said to her, Return to your mistress and submit yourself under her hands. **10** And the Angel of Jehovah said to her, I will multiply your seed exceedingly, so that it shall not be numbered for multitude. **11** And the Angel of Jehovah said to her, Behold, you are with child, and shall bear a son. And you shall call his name Ishmael, because Jehovah has heard your affliction.

I say a child as they were childless, and there was no way that either of them could have known if Hagar would produce a son or a daughter. A son was what Abraham wanted, as a daughter could not inherit. I will say this for Abraham's taking Hagar as a means of having a child, that the promise was that he would have a child from his own bowels or loins, and nothing was mentioned of Sarah. So this was a possible means of having a son and the fulfillment of the promise of a multitude of offspring. They were both very old and had not been successful in having a child. It was considered a shameful thing to not be able to have children. Here is the leader of the clan and his wife who are not able to conceive and have a child. It must have been difficult to live with. So since Sarah could not conceive, she suggested to Abraham that he go in to Hagar and through her they could have a child. Sarah told Abraham that now that Hagar has conceived, I am despised in her eyes. Abraham replies that it is her handmaid and she can do as she pleases with her. Sarah deals harshly with her. A child through her handmaid was not a blessing to Sarah, but was more of a curse to her. So in the end, according to the direction of the angel, Hagar returns to her mistress. Ishmael would not be the heir to Abraham, but Hagar would not be left without the promise of a great number of generations after her, through Ishmael. We do not know why Abraham did not seek the Lord about this issue or why God did not intervene and stop him from going into Hagar. We do know from the following scripture that God did intervene eventually, and the promise of a son to Abraham was again repeated.

Genesis 18:1 And Jehovah appeared to him in the plains of Mamre, and he sat at the tent door in the heat of the day. **2** And he lifted up his eyes and looked, and lo, three men stood by him. And when he saw *them*, he ran to meet them from the tent door, and bowed toward the ground. **3** And he said, My Lord, if now I have found favor in Your sight, do not pass away, I pray, from Your servant. **4** Let a little water, I pray, be brought, and wash Your feet, and rest under the tree.

5 And I will bring a bite of bread, and will comfort your hearts. After that You shall pass on. For this is why You have come to Your servant. And they said, Do so, as you have said. **6** And Abraham hastened into the tent to Sarah, and said, *Make ready* quickly three measures of fine meal; knead *it*, and make cakes. **7** And Abraham ran out to the herd and brought a calf, tender and good. And he gave *it* to a young man. And he hurried to dress it. **8** And he took butter and milk, and the calf which he had dressed, and set *it* before them. And he stood by them under the tree, and they ate. **9** And they said to him, Where *is* Sarah your wife? And he said, Behold, in the tent. **10** And He said, I will certainly return to you according to the time of life, and lo, Sarah your wife *shall have* a son. And Sarah heard in the tent door which was behind Him. **11** Now Abraham and Sarah *were* old, far gone in days, and it had ceased to be with Sarah after the manner of women. **12** Therefore Sarah laughed within herself, saying, After my being old, shall I have pleasure, my lord being old also? **13** And Jehovah said to Abraham, Why did Sarah laugh, saying, Shall I, who am old, truly bear a child? **14** Is anything too hard for Jehovah? At the time appointed I will return again, according to the time of life, and Sarah *shall have* a son. **15** Then Sarah denied, saying, I did not laugh; for she was afraid. And He said, No, but you did laugh.

I find it interesting that it was the Lord and two angels that visited Abraham. Later in history, the Lord told Moses that he could not see his face and live, and yet God spoke face to face with Abraham. I think it is amazing, that God actually appeared to him face to face. We know this happened from the following Scripture.

Genesis 17:1 And when Abram was ninety-nine years old, Jehovah appeared to Abram and said to him, I *am* the Almighty God! Walk before Me and be perfect. **2** And I will make My covenant between Me and you, and will multiply you exceedingly.

In Genesis 18:17, we have the account of the visit with Abraham from the Lord and two angels. And Jehovah said, *"Shall I hide from Abraham the thing which I do?"* Abraham does what is the custom of the day and has a meal prepared for his guests. Then the Lord asks where is your wife Sarah. Abraham says in the tent, and God once again gives them a promise of a son and says Sarah will become pregnant and that he will return the next year at the time of life. Abraham is one hundred years old and Sarah is ninety years old. They had waited for many years now for the promise of a son, and now once again the promise is repeated when they are too old to have a child. Sarah laughs at the thought of having a child when she is passed the stage of a woman being able to have a child. I do not think that it was a laugh of mockery, but at the seemingly impossibility of her now having a child. Her laughing must have been important because the Lord confronts it and asks why she laughed. She responds in fear at the confrontation and denies laughing. The Lord does not leave it there but says yes, you did laugh. Abraham, when first told by the Lord of this promise, laughed and said the following: Genesis 17:17 *And Abraham fell upon his face and laughed, and said in his heart, Shall a child be born to him that is a hundred years old? And shall Sarah, who is ninety years old, bear?* There did not appear to be any confrontation from the Lord about Abraham laughing, and I am not sure why the difference between his laughing and Sarah laughing. Whatever the case, Sarah does become pregnant. Ishmael is fourteen years old when Issac is born, and he and Hagar will be sent away eventually.

Their faith was tested as they had to believe, without seeing and without any natural possibility of what was promised ever happening. God could have easily caused Sarah to conceive while she was still young, and Ishmael would never have been born. Abraham obviously did not believe that God would give them a child through Sarah, as she was past the age of being able to conceive, or he would not have gone in to Hagar in an attempt to fulfill God's promise of an heir. In spite of his trying to work it out, God still kept His promise. The question that stands out was: Is anything too difficult for God? Abraham's faith would grow and his trust in God would also grow. True biblical faith is confidence and trust in God. This test of his faith would lead to the ultimate test of Abraham's faith and obedience to God. It would prove that he truly believed that nothing is too difficult for God. In the following scriptures, we have the account of the ultimate test of Abraham's faith.

Gen 22:1 And it happened after these things that God tested Abraham, and said to him, Abraham! And he said, Behold me. **2** And He said, Take now your son, your only one, Isaac, whom you love. And go into the land of Moriah, and offer him there for a burnt offering upon one of the mountains which I will name to you. **3** And Abraham rose up early in the morning, and saddled his ass, and took two *of* his young men with him, and Isaac his son. And he split the wood for the burnt offering and rose up and went to the place of which God had told him. **4** Then on the third day,

Abraham lifted up his eyes and saw the place afar off. **5** And Abraham said to his young men, You stay here with the ass. And I and the boy will go on to this way and worship, and come again to you. **6** And Abraham took the wood of the burnt offering and laid it on Isaac his son. And he took the fire in his hand and a knife. And they both went together. **7** And Isaac spoke to Abraham his father and said, My father. And he said, Here *am* I, my son. And he said, Behold the fire and the wood. But where is the lamb for a burnt offering? **8** And Abraham said, My son, God will provide Himself a lamb for a burnt offering. So they both went together **9** And they came to the place which God had told him of. And Abraham built an altar there and laid the wood in order. And he bound his son Isaac and laid him on the altar, on the wood. **10** And Abraham stretched out his hand and took the knife to slay his son. **11** And the Angel of Jehovah called to him from the heavens and said, Abraham! Abraham! And he said, Here *am* I.

12 And He said, Do not lay your hand on the lad, nor do anything to him. For now I know that you fear God, since you have not withheld your son, your only one, from Me. **13** And Abraham lifted up his eyes, and looked. And, behold, a ram behind *him* was entangled in a thicket by its horns. And Abraham went and took the ram and offered it up for a burnt offering instead of his son.

What an amazing request. Abraham waited until he was one hundred years old before finally receiving the promise of God for a son, and now God is asking him to take him, his only son, and offer him on the altar as a sacrifice. Issac was around twelve years old at this time. God does not mention Ishmael, as apparently He does not consider him a son and is speaking of Issac as Abraham's only son. Abraham does not hesitate in his obedience. We do not know if he told Sarah what was happening, but we do know that he did not tell Issac. I wondered what Abraham must have been thinking of such a request. Was he wondering how in the world God was going to keep his promise of multiplying his seed exceedingly? Who would be his heir if Issac is no longer his heir? We do not have to wonder; we can know from the book of Hebrews what he was thinking.

Hebrews 11:17 By faith Abraham, being tested, offered up Isaac. And he who had received the promises offered up his only-begotten *son*, **18** of whom it was said that in Isaac your Seed shall be called, **19** concluding that God *was* able to raise him up, even from *the* dead, from where he even received him, in a figure.

Although this is not the meaning of the raising from the dead, God had, in fact, already raised up Issac from the dead womb of Sarah. Three days' travel brought them to Mount Moriah. Issac is aware of the wood and the fire for the sacrifice, but He is wondering about the lamb. When he asks, Abraham says that God will provide the lamb. It sounds like a diversion from telling Issac that he will be the sacrifice. Sooner or later, this will become obvious, but Abraham is apparently not ready to tell him. When they reached the place where God had shown Abraham, he built an altar and prepared the wood. There appears to be no explanation; Abraham simply binds his son and lays him on the altar. Issac does not have to wonder any longer. What must he have been thinking? His obedience and lack of any resistance say a lot about his trust in his father. Abraham raises the knife to kill his only begotten son, and the angel of the Lord stops him. What the angel then says is strange to me. Why would the angel of the Lord need to know that Abraham would sacrifice his son? The scripture says that the angel of the Lord stopped him and then the angel says, "Now I know that you will withhold nothing from Me." The end of the statement says that you have withheld nothing from Me. The angel of the Lord? I wonder why the angel of the Lord would need to know. I know that God is aware of what is happening as He is the one who directed Abraham to offer up his son. Also, God knows all things, so why would He say now I know that you will withhold nothing from me. Since God knows all things, then He knew beforehand that Abraham would obey Him. Whatever the case, we do know that God knew what Abraham would do, so why the statement of "now I know." I think that what God knew now was more than foreknowledge. it was from an experiential relationship with Abraham. It was a knowing from the relationship and a walking it out with Abraham. The other one who was well aware that Abraham would withhold nothing from God was Issac. Under the influence of the Holy Spirit, the apostle Paul wrote the following statement about Abraham and his faith.

Romans 4:18 *For he* who beyond hope believed on hope for him to become the father of many nations (according to that which was spoken, "So your seed shall be"). **19** And not being weak in faith, he did not consider his own body already dead (being about a hundred years old) or the deadening of Sarah's womb.

Rom 4:20 He did not stagger at the promise of God through unbelief, but was strong in faith, giving glory to God, **21** and being fully persuaded that what God had promised, He was also able to perform.

Abraham was unaware that what God had requested of Him was prophetic. Some two thousand years later, Father God would give His only begotten son as a sacrifice for our sins. Just as Issac had obeyed his father, even unto death, so Jesus would obey His Father and surrender to the cross and die for us. What must have seemed like a strange thing to ask had far-reaching meaning. It was fitting for the father of our faith to establish what is now expected of us. We are to give our lives for the Lord. Throughout history, some even physically gave their lives for Him. Only God knows what lies ahead for each of us. By His grace, we can walk in faith and complete the path He has for us. The clear message from the father of faith is that faith is expected for those who accept God's forgiveness and salvation. We are to trust and have confidence in our heavenly Father and accept the path He has for our lives. The lies and accusations of the enemy have, for millions of people, distorted their view of who God is and His heart for us. Scripture is clear that salvation is not earned by works, but that works and a walk of faith are part of our walk with God. It is not simply a matter of fire insurance and escaping hell. God wants us to be a part of His family. The enemy would want us to believe that a loving God would not send anyone to hell. God did not create hell for people, but for the devil and his cohorts. God has done all He can to open the door for us to have a relationship with Him. What more could he do than to send His son to die for us? He has made it possible for us to return to paradise. It will not be a paradise here on this earth, but it will be in heaven, and heaven will be beyond what we can think or imagine.

Committing our lives completely to God and the Lordship of Jesus is not a commitment to a dictator but to a loving father and to the one who gave His life for us. God is not a user but a giver. We can see this from the following scripture.

Hebrews 11:6 But without faith *it is* impossible to please *Him*, for he who comes to God must believe that He is and *that* He is a rewarder of those who diligently seek Him.

We have already stated that simply believing that God exists does not equal salvation or make you a Christian. From this scripture, we see that without faith, it is impossible to please Him, and what we must also believe is that he is a rewarder of those who diligently seek Him. A rewarder and not a user. The Greek word for rewarder is misthapodotes and is defined as one who pays a good wage. Even though we owe Him everything, He does not take advantage of that and use us to serve Him but rewards us for our service. Just because we are in the family does not mean we do not get rewarded for our obedience and service.

Also, we are to grow in our faith. What does it mean to grow in faith? Simply put, to grow in faith means to grow spiritually. It is to mature in both knowledge of God and in godly living. Ultimately it means to become more like Christ. This was God's plan for us, that we would be conformed to the image of His Son Jesus. Just as a person grows physically from an infant to a mature adult, a Christian's life is designed to grow spiritually from baby to mature Christian.

We have seen from the life of Abraham that God did indeed reward him for his faith and obedience. What we also observed from Abraham was that he grew in faith. As He walked with God He learned that God was true to His Word, and it increased his faith. He started his walk with God by believing and therefore, obeying what God told him about leaving his homeland. He journeyed to the land that God directed him to go to. Then he learned that God could do the impossible and give him and Sarah a child in their old age. Finally, he had grown to the point that he could obey God in the most difficult of tests. He was to sacrifice his son Issac as an offering to God. He believed that God would be faithful to His promise and that God could raise Issac from the dead. The more we trust Him and walk in obedience, the more we will grow in our faith.

Another important thing to understand about faith is that it is not based on our own understanding. There are millions of things we do not understand. I do not understand how God can speak to millions of people at the same time. I know and believe that He can and does. I know this by faith and not based on my understanding of how He could possibly do so. How did He speak, and the world came into being? How big is the universe, and are there other life forms on some other planet? Why do the wicked seem to prosper and the righteous suffer? There are an endless amount of things we don't understand. I don't understand how I can sit at my computer and type and the words come up on a screen and then I can print them. My three sons all work in computer science areas, and when they get together and discuss their work, I don't have a clue what they are talking about. They might as well be speaking a foreign language. Our lack of understanding is a real weapon used by the enemy, as it gives him plenty of ammunition to question our faith. I don't understand the direction God gives me at times. My typical response when I was first saved, was to ask why. I want details and I want to know what the end is from the beginning, but I will really never know that. My trust and faith in Him cannot be based on my own understanding. I don't understand how I could be changed in a moment from the old man to a new creation. How did the old man die and I became a new creation? It was a miracle. I don't understand it, but I have lived it, and I know it is true. Most of my struggles with this area were lessened greatly when God led me to the following scripture.

Proverbs 3:5 Trust in Jehovah with all your heart, and lean not to your own understanding. **6** In all your ways acknowledge Him, and He shall direct your paths. **7** Do not be wise in your own eyes; fear Jehovah and depart from evil.

8 Healing shall be to your navel and marrow to your bones.

Some say hindsight is 20/20, and I would agree that it can be. I have wondered at God's direction many times, and in some cases when I have looked back, I could see what His purpose was and how things fit together. Some things I will likely never understand, but I trust Him, and when I hear and know His voice, I am not afraid any longer to take the path He is directing. At times the direction has been for correction, and the Word says that if we are not disciplined by the Lord then we are not His children. The Father corrects those He loves. God's discipline is a corrective action to prevent harm and to bless us, not to harm us. Discipline is not retribution. The following would be retribution: you disobeyed, and therefore, you are going to be punished. Granted, discipline is not pleasant when it is given, but if received, it will bring forth the fruit of righteousness.

Some years ago, I received the following word from the Lord. He told me not to put my faith in my love for Him but in His love for me. It was not how well I was loving him that increased and supported my faith. Knowing His love and basing my faith in His love delivered me from a lot of erratic faith. My love is not perfect and will never be perfect, but His love is, and His love and commitment to me is absolutely trustworthy. To walk daily with my loving Father has been a great blessing and a wonderful adventure. May you grow in your faith and finish the race set before you.

Chapter 8: War

One of the lies of the enemy we need to be aware of is the lie that once we are saved, our lives will be blessed and our problems will be over. That would be really great if it were true, but it is not; however, it will be true in heaven. Before we are born again, we are not a threat or a concern to the enemy. We are lost, and he can easily, at various levels with different people, deceive us to do his will. He is well aware that God loves everyone, so his attacks are not just against Christians. However, once we are saved, we become a definite target, and he will do whatever he can to fight against us. His motive is his hatred of our heavenly father. The truth is we are in a war. We become a part of God's family by our free choice, through salvation; however, being in the army of God is not a choice, we are automatically drafted. If you are a born-again Christian, you are in a war. According to the following verse, that war is not against flesh and blood.

Ephesians 6:12 For we do not wrestle against flesh and blood, but against principalities, against powers, against the world's rulers, of the darkness of this age, against spiritual wickedness in high *places.*

This rules out all humans since they are flesh and blood. It does not mean that our true enemy will never work through humans. He works through those who are not saved, and sadly, he also works through those who are saved. Not every negative thing that happens is necessarily an attack from the enemy, but the result of evil and sin in the world. Sometimes we are bringing negative things on ourselves as a result of our choices, and not every negative situation is a demon. One of the things experienced by those who go to war is the fear of death. Thankfully, in this battle, we do not have to fear death. The enemy cannot take our life, and the following verses declare it to be true.

Hebrews 2:14 Since then the children have partaken of flesh and blood, He also Himself likewise partook of the same; that through death He might destroy him who had the power of death (that is, the Devil), **15** and deliver those who through fear of death were all their lifetime subject to bondage.

Jesus destroyed the devil, who had the power of death. The Greek word for destroy is katargeo, and has the following definition: to cause to cease, put an end to, do away with, annul, abolish. Jesus defeated the devil and abolished his power over us. He is a defeated foe, and one day, He will be cast into a lake of fire, where he will be tormented forever. Then the battle will truly be over. He has no power or authority over us, and we do not have to fear death or the enemy. The only way he can affect our lives is through his lies and temptations to sin, and he can only gain access through the doors we open to him. We are to stand against and defend ourselves from the lies and temptations of the enemy. We are not to fear the enemy, and fear is actually demonic. If he could kill us, he would certainly do so. I thank God that I no longer fear the enemy. When I was first saved I did fear him. I remember wanting to obey the Lord, but just enough so I did not tick off the devil, as I did not want him to attack me. I believed a lie, and I lived the lie. God is the opposite of hate, and the scriptures tell us that God is love. In the book of First John, the Bible makes a statement about fear and love.

1 John 4:18 There is no fear in love, but perfect love casts out fear, because fear has torment. He who fears has not been perfected in love. **19** We love Him because He first loved us.

At the end of chapter 7 of this book, I said that God had told me that I should not put my faith in my love for Him, but in His love for me. I needed to grow in my understanding and experience of the love of God and understand that the biblical fear of God is a reverence for God and not a terror. We love Him because He first loved us, and it is through relationship with Him that we become more and more aware of His love and learn to trust and believe that He is faithful, and that we do not have to fear.

We do not fight alone, as we have the Lord who backs us up and will give us the strength and the wisdom to stand strong. The book of Ephesians 6:10 says, *Finally, be strong in the Lord and in his mighty power.* We do not fight in our own strength and we do not fight alone. Our battle is not just a defensive one, we are to take the offense and attack as well. The goal is lost souls brought to salvation. There is nothing on this earth that will remain; however, everyone will exist forever but only those who are born again will have eternal life. The battle continues, even though the power of the enemy is destroyed because God does not want anyone to perish, and so He is long-suffering. I am so thankful that the Lord did not return fifty-one years ago because I would have died in my sins and I would never have known Him. Rather than merely standing our ground against the attacks of the enemy, we are to attack and rescue those who are bound by his lies and deceitful ways. Jesus did not fight alone. He said that in and of Himself He could do nothing. He depended on the Father and the power of the Holy Spirit to finish the mission set before Him. Since Jesus could not fight on His own, we certainly cannot. We have the Holy Spirit living within us, and He is there to strengthen and guide us. The apostle Paul said in Philippians, *I can do all things through Christ who strengthens me.* We can do the same. We can stand against the lies, accusations, and temptations of the enemy by the Lord's power. We can also take the enemy's territory by sharing the gospel, loving people, and living our lives as an example. It is not our power that defeated the enemy, it was His power, and it is His power that will defeat him in our lives.

This battle is not a physical battle but a spiritual battle. The spiritual realm can certainly affect the natural, but the battle we are fighting is a spiritual battle. We do not fight against flesh and blood. At times we are trying to solve issues and attacks in the natural, and we should be fighting in the spiritual. We are all aware of the wars fought in the natural, and some of us fought in them. Some wars were fought in America and others were fought in other countries. Many lives were lost, but because of the soldiers that went to war, many lives were saved. We also have weapons, and they are spiritual and not physical. Our battle is more than an individual battle, and we need to go to war to save the lives of those who are lost. The following portion of scripture identifies the weapons of our warfare.

Ephesians 6:10 Finally, my brothers, be strong in *the* Lord and in the power of His might. **11** Put on the whole armor of God so that you may be able to stand against the wiles of the devil. **12** For we do not wrestle against flesh and blood, but against principalities, against powers, against the world's rulers, of the darkness of this age, against spiritual wickedness in high *places*. **13** Therefore take to yourselves the whole armor of God, that you may be able to withstand in the evil day, and having done all, to stand. **14** Therefore stand, having your loins girded about with truth, and having on the breastplate of righteousness **15** and your feet shod with the preparation of the gospel of peace. **16** Above all, take the shield of faith, with which you shall be able to quench all the fiery darts of the wicked. **17** And take the helmet of salvation, and the sword of the Spirit, which is the Word of God, **18** praying always with all prayer and supplication in *the* Spirit, and watching to this very thing with all perseverance and supplication for all saints.

The apostle Paul lists the natural weapons of warfare used in his time to illustrate the reality of our having weapons for the spiritual battle. He no doubt had the Roman soldier's armor in mind. Each piece of armor is important, and we are to put on all the armor. The armor is God's armor, not our armor, and He has prepared us for spiritual warfare. We are to put on all the armor He has prepared for us in order to stand against the wiles of the devil. The Greek word for wiles is methodeia, defined as cunning, deceit, craftiness, and trickery, which is his method of warfare. He does have a large number of cohorts, which are the rulers of darkness and wickedness in high places. The high places are literally the heavenly places, which is the sky or air. We are not fighting against flesh and blood! If we fight against each other, we must realize that we have been taken in by a diversion of the enemy. Flesh and blood, saved or not saved, is not our enemy! Satan is the accuser of the brethren and the one who works through those who allow him to do so. He is also the accuser of the ones who are not part of the brethren. He wants us fighting each other and not him and his cohorts. We are the army of God, and when we stand together, we increase our power over the enemy and defeat his efforts at trying to destroy us. We are to stand, but we do not to stand alone. What would happen if all true believers, separated by denominational doctrines, would stand together? Our power and effectiveness as the army of God would be increased dramatically. Jesus declares, in the following verses, that there is power in unity.

Matthew 18:19 Again I say to you that if two of you shall agree on earth as regarding anything that they shall ask, it shall be done for them by My Father in Heaven. **20** For where two or three are gathered together in My name, there I am in their midst.

Having done all to stand, stand therefore. To stand is to make firm, to establish. You need to know and understand your position in Christ and stand firm. The first piece of armor listed is the belt, and at that time, it was called a *girdle*. It was a leather belt worn on the outside of the armor and it had straps hanging from the front. Some of the straps would have little metal studs on them and decorative items on the bottom of the straps. The belt and the straps would provide some protection for the area of the loins. In the apostles' time, the men wore long flowing garments, but loose clothing was a hindrance to efficient movement, so they would raise their clothing and tuck it into their belt so they could move freely. The loins are the sides between the lower ribs and pelvis, and the lower part of the back. The loins are also the seat of reproduction and therefore, an instrument of life. In the spiritual sense, the loins are to be prepared with truth. The truths that will defend against the wiles of the enemy. The Christian soldier must be vigilant and always prepared and ready to do battle. A common expression in America has been the need "to roll up your sleeves" when hard work is necessary to accomplish a difficult task. This modern expression is the equivalent of the biblical expression of girding up the loins. The truth is to be biblical truth and not a matter of our personal opinion. Proverbs 14:12 says, *there is a way which seems right unto a man, but the end thereof are the ways of death.* Our friends are certainly willing to give us their opinions, but the truth is most opinions are a dime a dozen because they are void of responsibility. We are personally responsible for knowing the truth. Some would advise to follow your heart, but Jeremiah said the heart is deceitful above all things and beyond cure; who can understand it? The truths we are to use in preparation for battle are to be taken from the Bible, and we also have the Holy Spirit who is our instructor and guide. Jesus said that he was the truth, and with the relationship we have with Him, we can know the truth and walk in it. The Bible is God's Word, and God can not lie. All scripture is for our benefit for doctrine, reproof, correction, and instruction in righteousness. In the following portions of scripture, we are exhorted concerning the means of supply for the truth.

Numbers 23:19 God *is* not a man that He should lie, neither the son of man that He should repent. Has He said, and shall He not do it? Or has He spoken, and shall He not make it good?

John 14:6 Jesus said to him, I am the Way, the Truth, and the Life; no one comes to the Father but by Me.

2 Timothy 3:16 All Scripture *is* God-breathed, and is profitable for doctrine, for reproof, for correction, for instruction in righteousness, **17** that the man of God may be perfected, thoroughly furnished to every good work.

Psalms 1:1 Blessed *is* the man who has not walked in the counsel of the ungodly, and has not stood in the way of sinners, and has not sat in the seat of the scornful. **2** But his delight *is* only in the Law of Jehovah; and in His Law, he meditates day and night. **3** And he shall be like a tree planted by the rivulets of water that brings forth its fruit in its seasons, and its leaf shall not wither, and all which he does shall be blessed.

Next, we have the breastplate of righteousness. This righteousness is not from us but is a gift from God. If you are born again, it is vitally important that you understand that Jesus took our sins to the cross and that you have received the gift of righteousness from God. His Word declares that our righteousness is a gift. It is the lie from the devil when he accuses us of not being righteous because of our behavior, which we know is not perfect. The truth is that we can never become righteous through a change in our behavior.

2 Corinthians 5:21 For He has made Him who knew no sin, *to be* sin for us, that we might become *the* righteousness of God in Him.

Romans 5:17 For if by one man's offense death reigned by one, much more they who receive abundance of grace and the gift of righteousness shall reign in life by One, Jesus Christ.

The breastplate of righteousness in the natural, consisted of two parts. The breastplate was made of leather, bronze, or iron, with a similar plate covering the back. The two were connected by leather straps or metal bands. These draped over the shoulders, and there was also hinges on the right side. This armor protected the lungs and the heart. Our spiritual breastplate is not accessed by trying harder to perform righteous acts but by faith. When the enemy would assail us with our lack of righteous behavior, we are able to respond to the truth that we are righteous because God has made us righteous. It is not that behavior does not matter, as our behavior is to change, but through His grace and power working in us. The enemy's efforts to condemn us will not affect us if we stand in faith, knowing that we have the righteousness of

God as a gift. The Bible declares that there is no condemnation to those who are in Christ Jesus. The trap of behavior as a means of righteousness has two sides to it. One is that we are condemned because we are having a struggle with some sin through either omission or commission and, therefore feel condemned. The other side of the trap is to think of ourselves as doing really good and taking credit for the behavioral change, and becoming proud. Neither of these scenarios is beneficial and are not the breastplate of righteousness.

Next, we have our feet shod with the preparation of the gospel of peace. I do not know for sure, but it appears that Paul could have been referencing the next portion of scripture when speaking of the gospel of peace.

Isaiah 52:7 How beautiful on the mountains are the feet of him who brings good tidings, making peace heard; who brings good news, making salvation heard; who says to Zion, Your God reigns!

Continuing with the illustration of the Roman soldier, Paul uses their footwear. In Paul's day, the normal footwear was not like the soldier's. The regular people wore what would be similar to our flip-flops or sandals and were made of leather. Soldiers needed footwear that would not come off their feet easily and give them more sure footing. They actually wore what we might call boots. They were straps of leather that could be bound up and tightened. The bottom or soul of the boot was made of a double layer of leather, and they put hobnails in the soles, that acted as cleats. The cleats would give the soldier a degree of firmness as he faced an opponent.

Spiritually speaking, we are to walk in peace. As a reminder, we are to be strong with the Lord's strength and not our own. We are to put on God's armor and not our own, and we are to put on all of the armor. We are to have our loins gird with truth, and God's gift of righteousness and not our own. Likewise, it is the Lord's peace we are to have and not our own. In the book of John, Jesus encourages His disciples with the following, "Peace I leave with you, my peace I give unto you: not as the world gives, give I unto you. Let not your heart be troubled, neither let it be afraid." We are to walk in peace, His peace. What about times of trouble? The words of Jesus to His disciples were after He told them that He was going to be crucified and die and that He would be leaving. Certainly, they were troubled by this information, and yet Jesus says, "Do not be troubled." How is that possible? It is possible because it was not them working up peace, but it was a peace that Jesus would give them. The following portion of scripture tells us how this is possible.

Philippians 4:6 Do not be anxious about anything, but in everything by prayer and supplication, with thanksgiving, let your requests be made known to God. **7** And the peace of God which passes all understanding shall keep your hearts and minds through Christ Jesus.

The enemy would have us believe that we can only have peace in the absence of conflict, but it is not so. I do not know how God does it, and I guess that it's okay, since the scripture says that His peace passes all understanding. Our feet are to be shod with the gospel of peace. The gospel, the good news, is for everyone. No one is exempt from receiving the salvation that God provided. We may think that some people are beyond redemption, but that is a lie. The apostle Paul said that he was not ashamed of the gospel as it is the power of God unto salvation to everyone who believes. Paul, when he was still Saul, was actually putting to death the Christians and did so until the Lord confronted him on the road to Damascus. No one is in a category of being beyond redemption. In this world, we will have tribulations and trials, but we can have peace through it all.

We now have an exhortation to take up the shield of faith. In chapter 7, we covered the subject of faith, what it is, and what it is not. The central biblical theme for faith is confidence or trust, and the object of faith is God and His Word. Paul continues with the illustration of the armor of God and references faith as a shield. He qualifies this item by saying above all, which appears to place it as superior to the other pieces of armor. The more correct translation is in addition to all, which does not place the shield as superior to all other pieces of armor. The statement that the shield would extinguish all the fiery darts of the enemy is because their shields were not metal. Metal shields would divert the arrows or spears, but the metal shields did not come about until the Middle Ages, which began after the fall of the Roman Empire. Their shields were made of layers of laminate wood. The layers were glued together, and the wood was covered with fabric and hide and had brass or steel wrapped around the edges. In the back of the shield, there was a piece of metal called a boss, which was in the center of the back of the shield and had a handle to hold the shield. This would protect the hand if a spear or sword punctured the shield. The shield was about two and a half feet wide and four feet tall, so a soldier could crouch down and get behind the shield as well as carry it. The shield was painted red to represent the Roman god of war, called Mars. It also represented the reality that in battle, blood will be shed, so the shield was covered in a symbol of blood. If a flaming arrow or spear hit the shield and stuck, it would allow the flame to be extinguished. So, the shield of faith represents our faith in God and His promises. He will never leave nor forsake us. He does not change. We can trust His word as He never lies. He is for us, and if he is for us, who can be against us?

We do not fight against flesh and blood, so the enemy will attempt, through accusations and lies, to separate us from our brothers and sisters and cause us to fight against each other instead of fighting together. The Roman soldiers would use their shields in quite a remarkable way, which I think is a fitting illustration of the unity of the believers and the effectiveness of our standing together. There was a strategic move the Roman soldiers would use that in English we would call the tortoise or turtle move. The front line of soldiers would line up next to each other, and their shields would butt up against each other. In this way, they created a wall. Every subsequent soldier would line up behind the soldier in front of them, and raising their shield above the soldier in front of them, they would take a kind of squatting position. This would form a sort of roof resembling a turtle shell. Each row of soldiers would do this. Then the platoon would advance forward, protected from the fiery darts, and continue their forward movement, like a tank. We are the family of God, and we need to stand together in faith. We need to move forward against the enemy and hold up the shield of faith, which will extinguish the fiery darts of the enemy.

The helmet of salvation is next. If we do not understand our salvation, we are vulnerable to the enemy who loves to attack us. He wants to try and convince us that when we sin or make a mistake, we are too far gone and that we may have lost our salvation. He will also use an opposite attack and try to convince us that we are perfect just the way we are and that sin doesn't matter and that we do not need to grow. Also, he will try to convince us that we just need to do more good than bad to secure our salvation. All of these attacks are effective if we do not understand our salvation. Paul says to put on the helmet of salvation, and again reverts to the illustration of the Roman armor. The Roman helmet was quite sophisticated. It was called a *galea* (gay-lee-uh). It was made of bronze or metal and would glisten in the sun. There was a visor piece on the front, and in the back, there was an added section that jutted out. If the enemy attempted to attack the head, the sword would glance off the visor and off the back of the head protection and not penetrate the head or shoulder. The soldiers needed to hear the commands of their supervisors, so they cut out an area of the helmet that covered the ears. They put a visor of sorts over each ear so that they would not lose their ears to the sword. They also had hinged cheek guards so that when it was hot and they were not in battle, they could move them up out of the way. They could also lower them when in battle for extra protection for the face. Officers had a distinct emblem on the top of the helmet made of horse hair and dyed red so that the soldiers could visually see their commanding officers. In a spiritual sense, we are to put on the helmet of salvation, which means to have a clear understanding of what the Lord has done for us and what is expected from us. There is much more that is provided for us through salvation than the forgiveness of sins. We have healing, provision, guidance, peace, comfort, and fellowship with the Lord, just to name a few. The lack of understanding of our salvation can cause a considerable lack of stability and, in some cases, torment in our walk with the Lord. Although not a comprehensive list of assurances, hopefully, the following scriptures will help you understand the security of our salvation.

John 10:27 My sheep hear My voice, and I know them, and they follow Me. **28** And I give to them eternal life, and they shall never ever perish, and not anyone shall pluck them out of My hand. **29** My Father who gave *them* to me is greater than all, and no one is able to pluck *them* out of My Father's hand.

Philippians 1:6 being confident of this very thing, that He who has begun a good work in you will perform *it* until the day of Jesus Christ,

Romans 8:38 For I am persuaded that neither death, nor life, nor angels, nor principalities, nor powers, nor things present, nor things to come, **39** nor height, nor depth, nor any other creature, shall be able to separate us from the love of God which is in Christ Jesus our Lord.

The next weapon in our arsenal is the sword of the Spirit. This is a weapon that is both defensive and offensive. More than any other illustration Paul has used, we can identify the sword of the Roman soldier as both a weapon of defense as well as a weapon of offense. Paul takes some of his imagery from the Old Testament. In Isaiah 49:2, Isaiah says, *He made my mouth like a sharpened sword.* We know that words have power. The old expression, "Sticks and stones may break my bones, but names will never hurt me," is certainly not accurate. Words can be very hurtful and have the power to encourage or do harm. Someone who has been verbally abused can, at times, suffer more than if physically abused, although both abuses are terrible and cause considerable damage. Martin Luther King Jr., through words, raised a national conscience of the injustice and bigotry of racial prejudice, and he did so with words and not violence.

Paul identifies, through the sword, another part of the Roman soldier's physical armor, and the spiritual sword as the Word of God. Words are powerful, but none more powerful than God's Word. Reading and understanding the Word is absolutely critical in the warfare we face. The Bible says that Jesus was led by the Holy Spirit into the wilderness for the purpose of fasting and to be tempted by the enemy. After Jesus had fasted forty days and forty nights, Satan came to Him. The enemy, using distorted Bible references, tried three times to tempt the Lord in an effort to lead Him astray. In each case, the Lord answered with the accurate and powerful Word of God. His first attempt was to try and get the Lord to prove who He was by commanding that the stones be turned into bread. He tempted the Lord to use His power to meet His own personal needs, and after forty days of fasting, bread must have sounded pretty good. Jesus responds with, *it is written, man shall not live by bread alone, but by every word that proceeds out of the mouth of God.* Next, he took Him up into the holy city and sat him on a pinnacle of the temple, and said unto him, *If thou be the Son of God, cast thyself down: for it is written, He shall give his angels charge concerning thee: and in their hands they shall bear thee up, lest at any time thou dash thy foot against a stone.* Again he uses what the scripture says about Him to tempt Him to prove who He was. Jesus responds with, *it is written, you shall not tempt the Lord thy God.* Again, the devil took him up into an exceeding high mountain, and showed him all the kingdoms of the world, and the glory of them; and said unto him, *all these things will I give thee, if thou wilt fall down and worship me.* Satan is finally at the heart of the issue. His wanting to be God and to be worshiped got him thrown out of heaven. Then Jesus said unto him, *Get thee hence, Satan: for it is written, Thou shalt worship the Lord thy God, and him only shalt thou serve.* We need to realize that the enemy wants to draw us in, with the final goal of having us bow down and worship him. We need to do what Jesus did when we are tempted, we need to use the sword and command the enemy to leave. Jesus was certainly hungry and He was all alone and unknown, yet He would not lift himself up, and finally, He would not bow to the enemy, even to gain the whole world. In each temptation, the Word of God had the answer. The Word of God is our sword, a defensive weapon and an offensive weapon. God's Word will tell us what is true, and we can defend ourselves against lies and temptations of the enemy. The Word of God can also become a weapon of offense. Paul said that he was not ashamed of the Gospel as it was the power of God unto salvation. Our offensive action should be to deliver those bound by Satan and bring them into the family of God. We are to carry on the ministry of Jesus. In the book of Luke, we find the mission of Jesus, and our mission spelled out for us.

Luke 4:18 "The Spirit of *the* Lord *is* on Me; because of this He has anointed Me to proclaim the Gospel to *the* poor. He has sent me to heal the brokenhearted, to proclaim deliverance to the captives, and new sight to *the* blind, to set at liberty those having been crushed, **19** to proclaim the acceptable year of *the* Lord.

We have something God's people did not have during the times of the Old Testament. We have the marvelous gift of the Holy Spirit, whom the Father sent to live in us. We no longer have to go to another human being, such as a priest, to talk to God or to obtain direction or forgiveness. The Bible says that all will know Him, from the youngest to the oldest. The knowledge of God will be without distinction of age or station; however, knowing God will obviously necessitate being born again. Also, different from the Old Testament times, the reality is that they only had the written word called the logos. We have the Spirit of God living within us, and He can communicate to us a Rhema word or a living word. Mentioned in an earlier chapter, the Word of God is clear on God's direction concerning our lives and our behavior in this life, as well as many other things, but it does not give us specific directions. Where am I to live? What is my profession supposed to be? Who am I to marry? What is my calling? The Holy Spirit will speak to us and guide and direct us where the Bible is not clear on these questions. Also, He will teach us and reveal the meaning of the Written Word. Jesus said, *My sheep hear my voice, and they do not listen to another,* so we must be sure that what we hear from the Holy Spirit is really from Him. What we hear must not contradict the Bible. Not that the Holy Spirit would ever misguide us, but we may assume we hear what we truly have not heard, and if it does not line up with the logos, we can know for sure it is not from God. God will also confirm His direction. It is not that God did not give clear direction to people in the Old Testament. He certainly told Abraham to leave his country and that He would lead him. Also, the prophets had words from the Lord. The personal relationship with God was not by and large available in the Old Testament times. Both logos and rhema are the Word of God, but logos is God's Word recorded in the Bible, while rhema is the word of God spoken to us by the Holy Spirit.

The next thing mentioned in this section on the armor of God is prayer. Paul does not give a weapon of the Roman soldier as an example, but he still includes prayer as the wrap-up of this portion on the weapons of our warfare. I don't think that I ever thought of prayer as a weapon. Did the Roman soldiers pray? It appears that they did, as they might have a handful of deities and they would generally pray to their favorite deity. They also had formal prayers in formal ways and in formal ceremonies. How they prayed or what they asked for, I don't know, but they might as well have prayed to a tree or the dirt. They may have gotten some direction from a demon or two, but they certainly did not get any information from other gods, as there are no other gods. I'm sure they prayed to the god of Mars, as he was supposedly the god of war, and they would need that prayer often. I do know that prayer is communication with God, which involves both speaking and listening. I wonder at the public prayers I have heard throughout the years that every third or fourth word is Lord, or God, or Jesus, and continues throughout the prayer. God's name or Jesus, or whatever is used, is not to be used as repetition or punctuation. I think that it is a matter of religious prayer and perhaps different when alone with God. I don't mean to be critical, but I think an example of what I am speaking of would be my communication with my wife. She is the closest person to me on this earth and someone I love dearly. I am not sure what she would think if I said her name, wife, woman, friend, partner, etc., every two or three words. I also would listen if I am to communicate with her. The following scripture is Paul's words inspired by the Holy Spirit, with instructions on prayer.

Ephesians 6:18 praying always with all prayer and supplication in *the* Spirit, and watching to this very thing with all perseverance and supplication for all saints.

The first thing that stands out is the word always. It seems to be directing us toward constant and immediate prayer, and the Bible also says to go into your closet and pray. Your closet would be a private place. Next is to pray in the Spirit. Even in prayer, the Holy Spirit can lead us and direct us as to what issues to be praying about. Next is all prayer, formal, silent, vocal, secret, public, petition, and supplication, all prayer. Supplication involves making passionate, specific requests during times of deep need or desire, a crying out. We are to pray with perseverance and also for all saints. The Greek lexicon brings out the idea of prayer being with perseverance is praying obstinately. *Obstinately* is defined as stubbornly refusing to change one's opinion or chosen course of action, despite attempts to persuade one to do so. The enemy definitely wants to divert us from prayer. He will try to bombard you with thoughts drawing you away from prayer.

The book of Psalms has all kinds of prayers. Jesus' disciples asked Him to teach them how to pray, and Jesus gave the following instructions, followed with instruction on how to pray.

Matthew 6:5 And when you pray, you shall not be like the hypocrites. For they love to pray standing in the synagogues and in the corners of the streets, so that they may be seen by men. Truly I say to you, They have their reward. **6** But you, when you pray, enter into your room. And shutting your door, pray to your Father in secret; and your Father who sees in secret shall reward you openly. **7** But when you pray, do not babble vain words, as the nations. For they think that in their much speaking they shall be heard. **8** Therefore do not be like them, for your Father knows what things you have need of before you ask Him.

Jesus' instructions on how to pray are what we call the Lord's Prayer:

Matthew 6:9 Therefore pray in this way: Our Father, who is in Heaven, Hallowed be Your name. **10** Your kingdom come, Your will be done, on earth as *it is* in Heaven. **11** Give us this day our daily bread; **12** and forgive us our debts as we also forgive our debtors. **13** And lead us not into temptation, but deliver us from the evil. For Yours is the kingdom, and the power, and the glory, forever. Amen

I want to close this chapter with a word of encouragement. There are two amazing things about prayer that are described in the following verses.

Romans 8:34 Who *is* he condemning? *It is* Christ who has died, but rather also *who is* raised, who is also at *the* right *hand* of God, who also intercedes for us.

Romans 8:26 Likewise the Spirit also helps our infirmities. For we do not know what we should pray for as we ought, but the Spirit Himself makes intercession for us with groanings which cannot be uttered. **27** And He searching the hearts knows what *is* the mind of the Spirit, because He makes intercession for the saints according to *the will of* God.

Jesus and the Holy Spirit are interceding for us. I know that the Father will answer their prayers, and it is comforting to know that they are both praying to the Father for us.

Chapter 9: The Battlefield

We have established from scripture that if you are a born-again believer, you are in a war. Paul used the Roman soldier's armor to illustrate the weapons of our warfare; however, our battle is not to be fought with physical armor. We do not fight against flesh and blood, but against principalities, against powers, against the rulers of the darkness of this world, against spiritual wickedness in high places. Although there are a number of scriptures that talk about the mind as the battlefield, the following scripture is foundational to understanding that our mind is in fact, the battlefield.

Romans 12:2 And do not be conformed to this world, but be transformed by the renewing of your mind, in order to prove by you what *is* that good and pleasing and perfect will of God.

Let's review what was explained in chapter 2 concerning being born again and the path that follows. Before we are born again, we have a fallen nature and are dead in our trespasses and sins. We are spirit beings and have inherited a fallen nature from the sin of Adam and Eve. Our inherited fallen nature and our own sins have separated us from God. We still exist, as all people will exist forever. Through our separation from God, we are dead spiritually even though we are alive physically and will exist forever. Jesus paid the price for our sins on the cross, and when we are born again through the salvation He provided, we become a new creation. We are connected to God through the new birth and are a part of the family of God; we are His children. It is at the point of the new birth that we begin the journey of changing the old habits and behaviors of the old man, who is the one who programmed our minds. The old man is now dead, and we are alive in Christ. The process is described in the book of Ephesians.

Ephesians 4:22 For you ought to put off the old man (according to your way of living before) who is corrupt according to the deceitful lusts, **23** and be renewed in the spirit of your mind. **24** And you should put on the new man, who according to God *was* created in righteousness and true holiness.

Again, the renewal of the mind is identified as the process of putting off the old man and putting on the new man. This process is called sanctification, which by definition means to be set apart and reserved for holy use. Jesus said the following in the book of John: "Sanctify them through thy truth: thy word is truth." The objective of every believer should be to hastily pursue sanctification. Our behavior needs to line up with our new life and manifest our freedom from sin. We tend to look at the forgiveness of sin and not pursue the deliverance from sin, which was also provided through salvation. Repentance is a change of mind and direction, taking a 180-degree turn from the life we lived as the old man to the new life we are to live as a new creation. It is a decision to walk a new path through relationship with the Father. If the mind and the body were renewed at the time we were born again, then our work would be done, but that is not the case. We are secure in the salvation provided by the Lord's sacrifice, but the habits of the old man have to be done away with. The battle from the enemy is directed toward keeping us from changing our way of life. He does so by bombarding us with negative, evil thoughts and accusations. He cannot steal our salvation or take away our relationship with God, but He will attempt to lure us into sin and make us unfruitful in the work of the Kingdom. The biggest battle we face is the battle of the mind. The devil is a liar, and if you believe his lies, you will end up living a lie. His ability to lie and deceive is his strongest weapon against us. He accuses us through our thoughts. He reminds us of past failures and sins and condemns us. He does so not only against us but against each other by planting thoughts of condemnation, judgment, criticism, blame, and unforgiveness toward others.

Remember that sin is never a good thing, nor has it ever been. Jesus gave us His Word to help us understand the life we are to live and how to do so. Sin's power is broken, and we are, through His power and grace, able to live a godly life and live free from sin. Thank God we are forgiven; now let us boldly advance through the removal of sin and live our lives for God. In the book of James, we are exhorted to submit ourselves to God, resist the devil, and he will flee from us.

We are instructed, in the book of Romans, to not be conformed to this world. The Greek word for conformed is *suschematizo* and means to conform one's self, one's mind, and character to another's pattern. We are told not to be conformed to the pattern of the world but to be transformed by the renewing of the mind. Transformed is the Greek word *metamorphoo,* which means to change into another form, to transform, to transfigure. We are not to be conformed to the world as the old man was but to be transformed and changed into another form, and this is accomplished by the renewing of the mind. As a born-again believer, we have the Holy Spirit dwelling in our spirit, and we have the mind of Christ from the Holy Spirit. The mind of Christ is revealed to us from the Word and from the Holy Spirit, and we are to change our thinking, which will change our behavior to what the Bible says and not the world. This necessitates work on our part. We can easily identify the work of the enemy in our minds by God's Word and by the Holy Spirit. The Holy Spirit is the Spirit of truth, and God's Word is the truth. We can fight any and all the lies of the enemy through His Word and through the guidance and direction of the Holy Spirit. The Holy Spirit will guide us into all truth. The Bible says *My sheep know my voice, and they will not follow another.* We are also to walk in the Spirit and we will not fulfill the lusts of the flesh. If we walk in the Spirit, which means to follow and obey the Holy Spirit, we will be able to prove what is that good, and acceptable, and perfect will of God. The scriptures below clearly state this.

John 16:13 However, when He, the Spirit of Truth, has come, He will guide you into all truth. For He shall not speak of Himself, but whatever He hears, He shall speak. And He will announce to you things to come. **14** He will glorify Me, for He will receive of Mine and will announce *it* to you. **15** All things that the Father has are Mine. Therefore I said that He will take of Mine and will announce *it* to you.

2 Corinthians 10:3 For though walking about in flesh, we do not war according to the flesh. **4** For the weapons of our warfare *are* not fleshly, but mighty through God to the pulling down of strongholds, **5** pulling down imaginations and every high thing that exalts itself against the knowledge of God, and bringing into captivity every thought into the obedience of Christ;

We walk in the flesh because we have a body and mind of flesh, but we do not walk according to the leading or dictates of the flesh. We are to walk in the Spirit, according to his leading and prescripts. Our weapons are mighty through God, to the pulling down of strongholds. Strongholds are thought patterns that are programmed into our minds and control our actions. They are built there by repetition of wrong thinking and the resulting wrong actions. They are like a castle or fortress. The enemy tries to build these strongholds in our thinking and, therefore affect our actions. They are false reasonings and arguments by which the enemy endeavors to fortify his thoughts and opinions in our minds. We are to cast down imaginations and every high thing that exalts itself against the knowledge of God and bring into captivity every thought to the obedience of Christ. Every thought! Really? Yes, every thought! That is how important our thoughts are. We are able to know what is of God from His Word and from the Holy Spirit and identify the thoughts of the enemy. His Word is the sword of the Spirit. The following scripture is a wonderful description of the power, majesty, and effectiveness of His Word.

Hebrews 4:12 For the Word of God *is* living and powerful and sharper than any two-edged sword, piercing even to *the* dividing apart of soul and spirit, and of the joints and marrow, and is a discerner of the thoughts and intents of the heart.

Quick is defined as alive, living, and not dead. The Word of God is actually alive. The Bible is the living Word of God because it is the message given to us from the living God. Jesus is the Word and Jesus is alive. The Bible is the inerrant Word of God. The word inerrant means free from error or untruths. We should not underestimate the power of God's word! It is far more powerful than any of us could ever imagine. God's Word is so powerful that through His spoken words, the world came into existence. It was so powerful that by quoting the written word, Jesus resisted and overcame the devil. It is powerful enough to sustain the universe and keep it operating. He is upholding all things by the word of His power. The Word is sharper than a two-edged sword, and it is able to divide the soul from the spirit. In the following portion of scripture, we have Paul's prayer to God that the Thessalonians would be preserved blameless, spirit, soul, and body.

1 Thessalonians 5:23 And may the God of peace Himself sanctify you, and may your whole spirit and soul and body be preserved blamelessly at the coming of our Lord Jesus Christ. **24** Faithful *is* He who called you, who also will do *it*.

Once again, due to sin, we were separated from God, and prior to being born again, we were dead in our trespasses and sins. Through the new birth, we received eternal life. We became a new creation, and our spirit was made clean from all sin. The Holy Spirit could not live in our spirit that was contaminated by sin. Jesus paid the price for sin, enabling us to become a new creation with sin removed from us. Sin was removed from our spirit and not from our mind or body. The old man, a spirit being, died, and a new creation, a new spirit man, was born. The removal of sin from our minds and bodies is the process of sanctification, which is accomplished by the renewal of our minds. Through this process, we put on the new man and do away with the behavior of the old man. The salvation of our spirit and becoming a new creation is separate from the salvation of our mind and body, which is the process of sanctification.

We can get a clearer picture of the seriousness of sin from the Old Testament. Once a year, the Israelites would have what is called Yom Kippur, the day of atonement, and a sin offering would be sacrificed for the entire nation. The high priest would enter into the holy of hollies to make the sacrifice. A rope was tied around his ankle in case he had any sin in his life. If he had any sin in his life that had not been forgiven through sacrifices, he would drop dead. They had no way of going in and getting him, and would have to pull him out with the rope. Also, there were bells on the bottom of the priest's robe, which would indicate that he was still alive. One sin and he would drop dead. Sin could not dwell in the presence of God, and God would never dwell in the presence of sin. Not even one sin! Now, as a new creation, we can boldly enter the very throne room of grace and receive mercy and grace to help in time of need. We enter the throne room of grace spiritually and not physically. If sin entered into our spirits, the Holy Spirit would have to leave our spirit because of our sin and then return once we were forgiven. We would be back under the old system, separated from God by our sin, and an animal sacrifice would be required for the forgiveness of our sin. I know that this may sound like eternal salvation in the sense that we can never lose our salvation. I do not believe this, as there are scriptures that would contradict. We are not saved to continue in sin. Through the grace and power of God, we can live free from sin. We are to renew our minds to the law of God written in our hearts and in the Word. To think that I am saved and, therefore it does not matter how I live is a total misrepresentation of salvation. Since Jesus died to deliver us from sin and the penalty of sin, it would be ludicrous to think that sin does not matter now that I am saved. The penalty of sin, which is death, is still enforced. Jesus gave us eternal salvation not so that we could continue to sin, but salvation delivered us from sin's penalty and from the power of sin. We are clearly to live a righteous and holy life, and follow the will and purposes of God for our lives. We are to be conformed to the image of God's Son,

Jesus and Jesus lived a life free from sin. He never sinned! Why would we think that there was any benefit in any sin? Should we take advantage of our freedom and continue to sin, ignoring the horrific price that was paid for our forgiveness and freedom from sin?

I would like to share with you what has helped give me a basis of understanding as to how we live and function as human beings, and I believe it to be a correct perspective. God is a triune God, defined as Father, Son, and Holy Spirit. Each is a distinct being and the three are one, in perfect agreement and harmony. Scripture bears this out and speaks of the three as individuals. Jesus speaks of His Father and declares that He will send the Holy Spirit to dwell in us. God created us as triune beings as well. We have a spirit, a soul, and a body. The scripture reference in 1 Thessalonians confirms this. In earlier chapters, we saw from scripture that we are a spiritual being and that every human being is a spirit being and will exist forever. The difference between those who are born again and those who are not, is where we will exist. We have eternal life through the new birth and not just eternal existence.

I personally believe, not only that we are triune beings, but that each of the three areas, spirit, soul, and body, also have three parts. This makes us a triple triune being, if you will. Again, I am not trying to establish a theological or doctrinal basis for this, but merely giving what I believe to be true as a means of understanding the possible functioning of each area.

I will begin with the *three* parts of the spirit, which are intuition, conscience, and devotion. I would define i*ntuition* as the ability to understand or act without the need for conscious reasoning. It is the ability to hear God's voice in our spirit. We have the mind of Christ, and it is not our brain as our natural mind is carnal and hostile to God. The following verses state this.

Romans 8:7 because the carnal mind *is* enmity against God, for it is not subject to the Law of God, neither indeed can *it be*. **8** So

114

then they who are in the flesh cannot please God. **9** But you are not in the flesh, but in *the* Spirit, if *the* Spirit of God dwells in you. But if anyone has not *the* Spirit of Christ, he is none of His.

This distinctly says that those who are not born again cannot please God as they are in the flesh. Therefore, adherence to religious works is not a means of salvation, and those who are not saved are not pleasing to God, no matter how good their religious activities are. We are in the Spirit if we are born again. We are to be transformed by the renewing of the mind because it is carnal and against God and must be renewed. What we read in the Bible and what the Holy Spirit speaks to us is what our minds need to be renewed to.

Next is *conscience*. I believe that the conscience is a part of the Spirit and is part of the directive from the Spirit as to proper or improper actions or thoughts. It is defined as an inner feeling or voice viewed as acting as a guide to the rightness or wrongness of one's behavior. Following our conscience is a matter of walking in the Spirit by knowing His voice and direction of our thoughts and actions and obeying them. When we were dead in our trespasses and sins, we as spirit beings were affected by our sins and disconnected from God. The old man did not and could not give proper direction according to God's will for our lives, There are those who have no conscience and are unable to distinguish right from wrong and are labeled as sociopaths. Some believe that the conscience is a part of the mind, but the mind is carnal and not at all reliable for direction or discernment of what is right and wrong. It is at enmity against the Spirit of God and, therefore could never be a proper director of our thoughts and actions and must be controlled and directed by the Spirit of God.

Finally, we have the third aspect, which is *devotion*. Devotion is defined as love, loyalty, or enthusiasm for a person, activity, or cause. The mind is not capable of loving God or being loyal to Him and is an enemy of God. The scriptures say that those who worship God must do so in spirit and truth. Devotion is a spiritual ability. The Holy Spirit lives in our spirit, and we are able to be truly devoted to God, to love Him, and obey Him as an act of our spirit. The mind and body must line up with the direction of the Spirit of God and be transformed by its renewal.

Now, we will move on to the three parts of the soul. Remember that we are spirit, soul, and body. The three parts of the soul are mind, will, and emotions. Our mind is our means of thinking and directing our thoughts and actions. It is defined as our cognitive abilities, which are thinking, reasoning, remembering, imagining, learning, and speaking. Our will is our ability to make choices. We are able to direct our mind through our choices, determining what we will think, remember, imagine, and speak. Our will, or volition, is a vital part of our ability to walk according to the direction and leading of the Holy Spirit. We have a choice of what we believe and what we think about and what we speak. Our emotions are described as our feelings. Not the physical feelings of touch, pain, or pleasure, but the emotional reactions to our thoughts, such as sadness, joy, etc. There is no scientific consensus on a definition. The following is an adaptation from the Merriam-Webster dictionary; emotions are conscious mental reactions (such as anger and fear) subjectively experienced as strong feelings usually directed toward a specific object and typically accompanied by physiological and behavioral changes in the body. The feelings are strongly connected to our thoughts and are not to be followed. The world would say, "If it feels good, do it." Not good advice!

The body also has three parts, flesh, bone, and blood, and is affected by our thinking, emotions, and choices. Obesity or anorexia, just to mention one area as an example, are both affected by our thoughts and emotions that direct what we eat or don't eat, and therefore, affect our bodies. Our thoughts and our emotions can greatly affect our physical health and well-being. The body has no power to direct but is led and affected by our thoughts and actions.

Volition can affect our lives to varying degrees, for the good or for the bad. I mentioned earlier in the book that the scriptures declare that the Holy Spirit will guide us into all truth, and not all truth about the choices we make is in the scriptures. For instance, where should I live? Who should I Marry? Where should I attend church? etc. Who could possibly do better than the Holy Spirit with these major decisions? The Word will also direct our decisions in many ways, but we are still left with making the choice. Some of the saddest statements in life are, what if, and if only. Some choices can be changed and paths redirected, but some have consequences that are not changeable. They can be forgiven but still have devastating results. A good biblical example of this is King David. David did not go to war but stayed home instead. One day, as he went out to the roof, he observed a woman taking a bath, and she was very beautiful. He decided to pursue having sexual relations with her. The scripture records that David had nineteen sons by various women and one daughter, Tamar. He was not being deprived of sexual relations. I don't know if it was entitlement or something else that led him to decide he would have her; however, we do know from scripture that it was a very bad choice. There is no question as to whether he knew better, he did. He sent for her and slept with her, and she became pregnant. Now, he had to decide what to do about his sin. He decided to cover it, and sent for her husband Uriah, had him brought home, and suggested that he have some time with his wife. Uriah refused and slept with the servants. Uriah said he could not go to her since his men were on the battlefield and were not able to be with their wives. So David made another bad decision, he asked Uriah to stay another night and got him drunk, thinking he would then go to be with his wife, but he did not. When David discovered this, he called for his captain Joab, and said for him to put Uriah on the front lines of the hottest battle so that he would die. Another terrible choice. After Uriah's wife had spent her days of mourning, King David sent for her, and she came into his house and he married her. What David did displeased the Lord. David's lust led to adultery, and eventually led to murder, and finally to the death of their baby boy. You would think that David should have died as well, but God spared his life. God told him that evil would come to him due to his choices. His choices were forgiven, but they would cost him dearly. The irony in this account is that the righteous choice of Uriah produced his death, that is if his choice was a truly righteous choice, since he disobeyed the command of the king. If he had obeyed the King and gone into his wife, he may have lived and eventually come home to her. We do not know if he would have lived, but if he died in battle, it would not have been from the direction of King David, who was literally guilty of murder. Ironically, even though David sinned, Bathsheba got pregnant and had a son who became one of the greatest kings of Israel.

What we think is vitally important as our battleground is the mind. We do not know how long it took David to send for Bathsheba, but we do know that he did. He knew it was wrong and yet he gave in to what was for sure not pleasing to God, and evidently, he was not thinking about the cost. Proverbs 14:12 says, *there is a way which seems right unto a man, but the end thereof are the ways of death.* The pleasures of sin are temporary. Satan only deceives you by telling you what your flesh will enjoy; he doesn't tell you what you'll suffer! The scriptures are clear that we are to take every thought captive to the obedience of Christ. Every thought! There are also thoughts from the enemy that are not necessarily sinful but misleading. Our commitment to the Lord is to walk according to the path that the Holy Spirit leads and directs. It is not just the temptations to sin, but the effort of the enemy is also to lead us, or I should say to mislead us. Wrong thinking can lead us to sin or to walk a path that is contrary to the one the Lord has for us.

In the battle of the mind, it is not enough to simply fight the wrong thoughts; we need to replace the wrong thoughts with the right ones. The lies need to be confronted with the truth. One of the major attacks of the enemy is to deceive us into thinking that the wrong thoughts are our thoughts. Some indeed have been programmed over years, and they are literally the thoughts of the old man who is now dead. However, the mind has to be renewed. There are also current thoughts that are not our thoughts but are from the enemy, and the battle of the mind will continue until we get to heaven. As stated in a previous chapter, we are a new creation, and the thoughts toward sin are not a part of our new nature; and in fact, they are actually contrary to who we are now. If the devil can convince you that the desires toward sin are actually your desires and not his temptations working through the flesh, which is the pathway he uses, then he will lead you into the sin and then condemn you for sinning. One of the big lies is that we can justify our sin, as it is not as bad as the sins of someone else. Also, we tend to categorize sin as not so bad or really bad. If I look at porn, it is not as bad as committing adultery, but in fact it is committing adultery. It is adultery if you are married and fornication if you are single. Sin never satisfies, and it will lead to what we may classify as worse sins. Another lie is that thoughts do not matter, they are just thoughts. As long as I don't make them known or act on what I am thinking, they are just thoughts and are not hurting anyone. The scriptures do not separate thoughts from actions. A wrong thought is a wrong action, even if it is just a "thought." The Bible says every thought is to be brought into obedience unto Christ. Wrong thoughts are wrong period! If we do not see the mind as the battlefield we can easily mistake the seriousness of our thoughts and excuse them as no big deal. I am going to share a personal experience in this area and the wake-up call that resulted from it. I was actually thanking the Lord one night that I had never been involved in porn. The Lord said what about the thoughts and the videos I play in my mind. I was shocked to realize that the thoughts were porn. I cried out, oh Jesus, please forgive me, and the battle of the mind became much more serious. I was actually sinning in my mind because I was willingly entertaining thoughts that I never should have entertained, but I thought they were just thoughts and really did no harm. Had

I not seen this I am certain that I would have eventually opened the door to actual pornographic material. The good news is that through the truth of God's Word and by His grace, I overcame the thoughts and won the battle.

I really like playing golf, and I also like watching the pro golfers on television. I try to watch them whenever I can, but at times I would have to work and was not able to. So I would record the tournament so I could still watch it later. I was really anxious and had a difficult time waiting to see if my favorite player won, so I would eventually give in and look online to see who won. I still was able to watch the tournament when I got home, but if my favorite guy did not win, I was disappointed. It was different watching a recording, knowing who won, as watching when I didn't know. Knowing made things a lot less tense. It was a totally different experience when I knew who won. I could see my favorite player have a bad shot, and it did not affect me the same as I knew it did not matter since he won. Knowing that we are in a battle and knowing who wins is a lot different from not knowing. It is a lot less stressful. We know that we are in a battle, but we know that Jesus has already defeated the enemy. We have been given inside information from the Bible. The attacks come, but I know that in Him and through Him the battle is already won. In fact, you can even rest and be at peace in the battle knowing the outcome is victory. No matter what mistakes, we make we know who won and who fights with us. Fighting a battle that, by His power and His strength, has already been won is a lot different than thinking you might lose the battle.

I would like to share another personal testimony. For a number of years, I had repeated terrifying occurrences over the fear of dying. For me, it was an awful struggle. I dreaded going to bed, as the fear of dying would be on my mind and torment me. I remember as a young boy, going to bed, and as I started to dose off, I remembered I had not prayed. I jumped out of bed and hit my knees, begging God not to kill me for forgetting to pray. I do not know what caused such fear, but I do know it was very real. The fear of dying troubled me for many years, and it was a terrible bondage. I am not sure if I knew that I was in a battle or that I would have called it that, but I was sure that I might not make it through the night. What a difference it would have made had I known that the battle was won. Once again, it was the Word and the grace of God that led me to the truth and set me free from the fear of death. The following scriptures were my sword, and my faith was a shield against the fiery darts of the enemy.

Hebrews 2:14 Since then the children have partaken of flesh and blood, He also Himself likewise partook of the same; that through death He might destroy him who had the power of death (that is, the Devil), **15** and deliver those who through fear of death were all their lifetime subject to bondage.

Philippians 4:4 Rejoice in *the* Lord always. Again I say, Rejoice! **5** Let your moderation be known to all men. The Lord *is* at hand. **6** Do not be anxious about anything, but in everything by prayer and supplication, with thanksgiving, let your requests be made known to God. **7** And the peace of God which passes all understanding shall keep your hearts and minds through Christ Jesus.

I now knew that Jesus had won the battle, and that the one who had tormented me with death threats all those years did not have the power of death. When the fear of death thoughts would come, I would simply stand against them, declaring to the enemy that he did not have the power of death and that he could not kill me. I said even if you could, it would be a win-win. If I live, I will live for the Lord and walk with Him, and if I die, I will be with Him in heaven. How can I lose? The battle is won, and I know who won. The mind is the battlefield, and whoever controls the mind will have control of the body as well. The mind is the battlefield, and through the Word and the leading of the Holy Spirit, we can in fact, fight the good fight.

Isaiah 26:3 You will keep *him* in perfect peace, whose mind *is* stayed on You; because he trusts in You.

2 Corinthians 10:5 pulling down imaginations and every high thing that exalts itself against the knowledge of God, and bringing into captivity every thought into the obedience of Christ;

Every thought! Did the Lord actually mean every thought? Yes! Why is it so important to bring every thought into obedience? Because our thoughts are the battlefield, and if we are to fight, we must fight on the battlefield. I will close this chapter with a final exhortation concerning our words and our thoughts.

Philippians 4:8 Finally, my brothers, whatever things are true, whatever things *are* honest, whatever *things are* right, whatever *things are* pure, whatever *things are* lovely, whatever *things are* of good report; if *there is* any virtue and if *there is* any praise, think on these things.

Chapter 10: Ripped Off

What I mean by ripped off is to have something stolen or to pay for something that is not worth what you paid for it. I said in the last chapter that there are no sadder words than, if only, or what if, and these have to do with choices made. Choices chart the path of our lives. Our choices take us somewhere, and the path you take is where you will end up. Every path has a destination that will take you somewhere sooner or later. We all make choices in this life and those choices have varying degrees of results. It may not be just one choice but a continuation of choices. Some choices actually become ruts, and they can be good ruts or bad ruts. Choices can have painful results and in some cases, very serious consequences. Choices can also bring good results and blessings. Some may have immediate results while others may produce later results. One thing is for sure, choices will produce results.

Do we really need to make bad choices? There is a choice that can change the entire path of your life and result in great blessing here on this earth and in the afterlife. This is the main point I want to make. This choice will affect your eternal destiny. I have explained how religious activities, as a means of salvation, is a really big rip-off. Choosing to live your life for yourself will not be worth the price you will pay for it. Who else but God could possibly do better at helping us to make the right choices? Could anyone make better choices than a loving Father who knows all things and wants to walk with us and lead us on the right path? Can you imagine people who thought they had purchased their salvation by good works and religious activities, to finally discover that they have made a wrong choice? Even people who are not bad people but have just made a bad choice. I can hardly bear to think about it. God loved them so much that He sent His only begotten son to purchase for them a salvation that would deliver them from sin and death and make them His children. It is the work of the enemy, who through deception, has managed to lead them down a deadly path. There are those also who have chosen a very evil path and will pay a horrendous price for it. The reality is that choices can produce a very critical difference. The following scripture identifies the character of the evil one, or I should say the demonic character of the evil one. He is a major rip-off con artist. In contrast, Jesus came that we might have life and have it more abundantly.

John 10:10 The thief does not come except to steal and to kill and to destroy. I have come so that they might have life, and that they might have *it* more abundantly.

The word abundantly in the *Greek* is perissos and means: over and above, more than is necessary, super added, exceeding abundantly, extraordinary, surpassing, and uncommon. Will we choose to walk a path following the enemy, who came to steal, kill, and destroy? You may think that you choose to live your own life and do whatever it is that you want to do, but the truth is that you have left an open door to the enemy, and he will lead you down a path of destruction and will not ask your permission. You are being ripped off!! The following scripture gives us the truth and reveals the possibility and the means of making good choices. We can trust the Lord with all our heart and not lean on our own understanding because the Bible directs us to, and therefore, by His power and grace, we can.

Proverbs 3:5 Trust in Jehovah with all your heart, and lean not to your own understanding. **6** In all your ways acknowledge Him, and He shall direct your paths. **7** Do not be wise in your own eyes; fear Jehovah and depart from evil.

How many ways does God want to lead and guide our decisions and the path we take in this life? The scripture above says in all your ways. The thing we are directed not to do is lean on our own understanding. We are not to put our faith in our own understanding but trust in the Lord to lead us. Fear the Lord, which means to have a reverence for the Lord, and turn away from evil.

God will not force you to listen to Him, and He will not take over your life and make you His slave. He loves us and wants to help us make the right choices and take the right path. This is the message of the following scripture.

John 16:13 However, when He, the Spirit of Truth, has come, He will guide you into all truth. For He shall not speak of Himself, but whatever He hears, He shall speak. And He will announce to you things to come.

He will send the Holy Spirit to live in us, and He will guide us into all truth. Not just theological truths, but all truth. Even the areas that the Bible does not spell out for us. Oftentimes we live our lives well below what is possible and miss the blessings of the Lord. We do so by making our own decisions and not following the path of the Holy Spirit. I believe that, even though we do not lose our salvation, much of what should be and could be is stolen from us as a result of our making independent choices. We do not know what lies ahead or what our decisions will produce. However, we can follow the leading of the one who does know, and we can make the right decisions by walking according to His leading. We may have different callings, but the callings that are important for us are the ones the Lord is calling us to. I want to share some testimonies of the outcome of choices, one negative decision from my personal life, a positive one from another person's life, and finally a biblical example.

One day, I was driving my son's car and pulled into the drive at my home. I needed to get something from the house, and when I came back out to get in the car, I clearly sensed that I should take my own car and not my son's. I ignored the prompting as I did not want to take the time to change cars. Some three miles from my home, I hit a deer and wrecked his car. The change in cars would have changed the timeline and the resulting impact, and I believe that it would have saved me from the accident. It was one of those times when I knew for sure what I should do but disobeyed. I did not like the results. I was free to choose, but my choice was to ignore the promptings of the Holy Spirit.

I think that most of the readers will be familiar with the name Billy Graham. A worker on the Graham farm named Albert McMakin, persuaded Billy to go and see the evangelist, Mordecai Ham, and he therefore attended the revival meetings. According to Billy Graham's autobiography, he was sixteen when he was converted during those revival meetings that Ham led in Charlotte in 1934. Ham had no idea that his messages in the revival would lead to the salvation of one of the greatest evangelists of our time. Literally hundreds of thousands of lives were affected by Billy Graham's ministry. Albert, the farmhand, also had no idea that his urging Billy to go to the meetings would have such an enormous impact on so many lives. Obviously, our choices may never have such an impact, but in reality, we do not know. We may need to take the road less traveled but end up at the right destination if we follow the one who knows all things and for whom all things are possible.

One of my favorite books of the Old Testament is the book of Esther. It is a tremendous testimony to the power of choices and the results of following the directions of the Lord. It also shows that God was working behind the scenes and that what appeared to be a disaster turned out to be a deliverance. I think that the only way I can present this account properly is to copy it from the Bible and allow the readers to read it for themselves. I want to be sure that it is portrayed accurately. I know that it is quite a bit of reading, but I do believe it is essential to understanding that some decisions have very serious results, and others can also hold great blessings. Also, that the one Who knows all things can lead us to the right choices even when we really do not have a clue of the outcome. In this portion, it is clear that they did not have any indication of what was ahead of them. The scriptures are copied from the American Standard Version.

Esther 3:1 After these things, King Ahasuerus promoted Haman the son of Hammedatha the Agagite, and advanced him, and set his seat above all the princes who *were* with him. **2** And all the king's servants in the king's gate bowed and worshiped Haman, for the king had so commanded concerning him. But Mordecai did not bow nor worship. **3** And the king's servants in the king's gate said to Mordecai, Why do you transgress the king's command? **4** And it happened when they spoke daily to him, and when he did not listen to them, they told Haman to see if Mordecai's matters would stand. For he had told them that he *was* a Jew. **5** And when Haman saw that Mordecai did not bow nor worship him, then Haman was full of wrath. **6** And he scorned to lay hands only on Mordecai, for they had revealed to him the people of Mordecai. And Haman sought to destroy all the Jews throughout the whole kingdom of Ahasuerus, the people of Mordecai. **7** In the first month, that *is*, the month Nisan, in the twelfth year of King Ahasuerus, they cast Pur, the lot, before Haman from day to day, and from month to month, to the twelfth *month*, the month Adar. **8** And Haman said to King Ahasuerus, There is a certain people scattered abroad and dispersed among the people, in all the provinces of your kingdom. And their laws *are* different from all people, neither do they keep the king's laws. And it is not for the king's gain to allow them to live. **9** If it pleases the king, let it be written that they may be destroyed. And I will pay ten thousand talents of silver to the hands of those who have charge of the business, to bring *it* into the king's treasuries. **10** And the king took his ring from his hand and gave it to Haman the son of Hammedatha the Agagite, the Jews' enemy. **11** And the king said to Haman, The silver *is* given to you, the people also, to do with them as seems good to you. **12** Then the king's scribes were called on the thirteenth day of the first month, and there was written according to all that Haman had commanded to the king's lieutenants, and to the governors *who were* over every province, and to the rulers of every people of every province, according to the writing of it, and to every people according to their language. It was written in the name of King Ahasuerus and sealed with the king's ring. **13** And the letters were sent by postal riders into all the king's provinces, to destroy, to kill, and to cause to perish, all Jews, both young and old, little children and women, in one day, on the thirteenth of the twelfth month, which is the month Adar, and *to take* what they owned for a prize. **14** The copy of the writing, for a command to be given in every province, was published to all people, to be ready for that day. **15** The posts went out, being hurried by the king's command, and the decree was given in Shushan the palace. And the king and Haman sat down to drink, but the city Shushan was perplexed.

Esther 4:1 And Mordecai understood all that was done, and Mordecai tore his clothes and put on sackcloth with ashes and went out into the middle of the city, and cried with a loud and bitter cry. **2** And he even came before the king's gate for none *might* enter into the king's gate clothed with sackcloth. **3** And in every province, wherever the king's command and his decree came, there *was* great mourning among the Jews, and fasting, and weeping and wailing. And many lay in sackcloth and ashes. **4** And Esther's servant women and her eunuchs came and told her. And the queen was exceedingly grieved, and she sent clothing to clothe Mordecai and to take away his sackcloth from him. But he did not receive *it.* **5** And Esther called for Hatach, *one* of the king's eunuchs whom he had appointed to attend on her, and gave him a command to Mordecai to know what it *was* and why it *was.* **6** And Hatach went forth to Mordecai, to the street of the city in front of the king's gate. **7** And Mordecai told him of all that had happened to him, and of the sum of the silver which Haman had promised to pay to the king's treasuries for the Jews in order to destroy them. **8** Also, he gave him the copy of the writing of the decree which *was* given at Shushan in order to destroy them, to show *it* to Esther and to declare it to her, and to command her that she should go in to the king to make supplication to him, and to seek help for her people. **9** And Hatach came and told Esther the words of Mordecai. **10** Again Esther spoke to Hatach and gave him command to Mordecai. **11** And the king's servants and the people of the king's provinces know that whoever, whether man or woman, shall come to the king into the inner court, who is not called, *there is* one law of his, execution, except such to whom the king shall hold out the golden scepter so that he may live. But I have not been called to come in to the king these thirty days. **12** And they told Mordecai Esther's words. **13** And Mordecai commanded them to answer Esther, Do not think within yourself that you shall escape in the king's house more than all the Jews. **14** For if you are completely silent at this time, relief and deliverance shall arise to the Jews from another place, but you and your father's house shall be destroyed. And who knows whether you have come to the kingdom for a time like this? **15** And Esther said to return to Mordecai *this answer,* **16** Go, gather all the Jews who are present in Shushan, and fast for me, and do not eat nor drink three days, night or day. My maidservants and I will also fast in the same way. And so I will go in to the king, which *is* not according to the law. And if I perish, I perish. **17** And Mordecai passed over and did according to all that Esther had commanded him.

Esther 5:1 And it happened on the third day, Esther put on royal *clothing* and stood in the inner court of the king's house, across from the king's house. And the king sat on his royal throne in the royal house, across from the gate of the house. **2** And it happened when the king saw Esther the queen standing in the court, she received favor *in* his sight. And the king held out to Esther the golden scepter in his hand. And Esther drew near and touched the top of the scepter. **3** And the king said to her, What do you *desire,* Queen Esther? And what *is* your wish? It shall be given to you even to half of the kingdom. **4** And Esther answered, If *it is* good to the king, let the king and Haman come today to the banquet which I have prepared for him. **5** And the king said, Cause Haman to hurry so that he may do as Esther has said. And the king and Haman came to the banquet which Esther had prepared. **6** And the king said to Esther at the banquet of wine, What *is* your petition that it shall be granted to you? And what *is* your request? It shall be performed even to half of the kingdom. **7** And Esther answered and said, *As to* my petition and my request, **8** if I have found favor in the sight of the king, and if it pleases the king to grant my petition and to perform my request, let the king and Haman come to the banquet which I shall prepare for them, and I will do tomorrow as the king has said. **9** And Haman went forth that day joyful and with a glad heart. But when Haman saw Mordecai in the king's gate, that he did not stand up nor move for him, he was full of fury against Mordecai. **10** But Haman held himself in. And when he came home, he sent and called *for* his friends and Zeresh his wife. **11** And Haman told them of the glory of his riches, and his many sons, and all to which the king had promoted him, and how he had advanced him above the princes and servants of the king. **12** And Haman said, Yes, Esther the queen let *no man* but me come in with the king to the banquet that she had prepared. And also tomorrow I am invited to *her banquet*, with the king. **13** Yet all this avails me nothing as long as I see Mordecai the Jew sitting at the king's gate. **14** And Zeresh his wife and all his friends said to him, Make a wooden *gallows*, fifty cubits high and tomorrow speak to the king that Mordecai may be hanged on it. Then go in merrily with the king to the banquet. And the thing pleased Haman, and he caused the wooden *gallows* to be made.

Esther 6:1 On that night the king could not sleep, and he commanded to bring the Book of the Records of the Matter of the Days. And they were read before the king. **2** And it was found written that Mordecai had told of Bigthana and Teresh, two of the king's eunuchs, the keepers of the door who tried to lay a hand on King Ahasuerus. **3** And the king said, What honor and dignity has been done to Mordecai for this? And the king's servants who served him said, Nothing has been done for him. **4** And the king said, Who *is* in the court? And Haman had come into the outer court of the king's house to speak to the king to hang Mordecai on the wooden *gallows* which he had prepared for him. **5** And the king's servants said to him, Behold, Haman stands in the court. And the king said,

Let him come in. **6** So Haman came in. And the king said to him, What shall be done to the man whom the king delights to honor? And Haman thought in his heart, To whom would the king delight to do honor more than to myself? **7** And Haman answered the king, For the man whom the king delights to honor, **8** let the royal clothing be brought, which the king wears, and the horse that the king rides on, and the royal crown which is set on his head. **9** And let this clothing and horse be delivered to the hand of one of the king's most noble princes so that they may dress the man whom the king delights to honor, and bring him on horseback through the streets of the city, and proclaim before him, This is what shall be done to the man whom the king delights to honor. **10** And the king said to Haman, Make haste! Take the clothing and the horse, as you have said, and do even so to Mordecai the Jew, who sits at the king's gate. Do not fail to do any of all the things you have spoken. **11** And Haman took the clothing and the horse and dressed Mordecai, and brought him on horseback through the street of the city, and proclaimed before him, This is what shall be done to the man whom the king delights to honor! **12** And Mordecai came again to the king's gate. But Haman hurried to his house mourning and having *his* head covered. **13** And Haman told Zeresh his wife and all his friends everything that had happened to him. Then his wise men and Zeresh his wife said to him, If Mordecai is of the seed of the Jews, before whom you have begun to fall, you shall not prevail against him but shall surely fall before him. **14** And while they *were* still talking with him, the king's eunuchs came. And they hurried to bring Haman to the banquet which Esther had prepared.

Esther 7:1 And the king and Haman came to the banquet of Esther the queen.

2 And the king said again to Esther on the second day of the banquet of wine, What *is* your petition, Queen Esther, that it may be granted you? And what *is* your request? And it shall be performed, even to the half of the kingdom. **3** And Esther the queen answered and said, If I have found favor in your sight, O king, and if it pleases the king, let my life be given me at my petition, and my people at my request. **4** For we are sold, my people and I, to be destroyed, to be killed, and to perish. But if we had been sold for men-slaves and women-slaves, I would have held my tongue, although the enemy could not make up for the king's damage. **5** And King Ahasuerus answered and said to Esther the queen, Who *is* he, and where *is* the one who dares presume in his heart to do so? **6** And Esther said, The man who is our adversary and enemy *is* this wicked Haman. And Haman was afraid before the king and the queen. **7** And the king, arising from the banquet of wine in his wrath, *went* into the palace garden. And Haman stood up to beg for his life from Esther the queen, for he saw that evil was determined against him by the king. **8** And the king returned out of the palace garden into the place of the banquet of wine. And Haman had fallen on the bed on which Esther *was*. And the king said, Will he also force the queen before me in the house? As the word went out of the king's mouth, they covered Haman's face. **9** And Harbonah, one of the eunuchs, said before the king, Also look! the wooden *gallows* fifty cubits high which Haman made for Mordecai, who had spoken good for the king, stands in the house of Haman. Then the king said, Hang him on it! **10** And they hanged Haman on the wooden *gallows* that he had prepared for Mordecai. And the king's wrath lay down.

Esther 8:1 On that day King Ahasuerus gave the house of Haman, the Jews' enemy, to Esther the queen. And Mordecai came before the king, for Esther had told what he *was* to her. **2** And the king took off his ring, which he had taken from Haman, and gave it to Mordecai. And Esther set Mordecai over the house of Haman. **3** And Esther spoke yet again before the king, and fell down at his feet, and begged him with tears to put away the evil of Haman the Agagite, and his plot which he had plotted against the Jews. **4** Then the king held out the golden scepter toward Esther. And

Esther arose and stood before the king, **5** and said, If it please the king, and if I have found favor in his sight, and if the thing *is* right before the king, and if I am pleasing in his eyes, let it be written to bring back the documents (a sly plan by Haman the son of Hammedatha the Agagite) which he wrote to destroy the Jews in all the king's provinces. **6** For how can I bear to see the evil that shall come on my people? Or how can I endure to see the slaughter of my kindred? **7** And King Ahasuerus said to Esther the queen and to Mordecai the Jew, Behold, I have given Esther the house of Haman, and have hanged him on the wooden *gallows*, because he laid his hand on the Jews. **8** And you write for the Jews as it pleases you, in the king's name, and seal *it* with the king's ring. For the writing which is written in the king's name and sealed with the king's ring, no man may turn back. **9** Then the king's scribes were called at that time in the third month, the month Sivan, on the twenty-third of it. And it was written according to all that Mordecai commanded to the Jews, and to the lieutenants and the governors and rulers of the provinces from India to Ethiopia, a hundred and twenty-seven provinces, to every province according to the writing of it, and to every people in their writing, and to the Jews according to their writing and according to their language. **10** And he wrote in the name of King Ahasuerus and sealed *it* with the king's ring. And he sent letters by riders on horseback, riders on royal steeds, stallions, even sons of mares. **11** In *them* the king granted the Jews in every city to gather themselves, and to stand for their life, to destroy, to kill, and to cause to perish, all the power of the people and province who desired to attack them, little ones and women, and *to take* what they owned for a prize, **12** on one day in all the provinces of King Ahasuerus, on the thirteenth of the twelfth month, which *is* the month Adar. **13** The copy of the writing for a command to be given in every province *was* announced to all people, even that the Jews should be ready against that day to avenge themselves on their enemies. **14** The runners, riders on stallions, royal steeds, went out, being hurried and pressed on by

133

the king's command. And the order was given at Shushan the palace. **15** And Mordecai went out from the presence of the king in royal clothing of blue and white, and with a great crown *of* gold, and with a garment of fine linen and purple. And the city of Shushan rejoiced and was glad. **16** The Jews had light and gladness and joy and honor. **17** And in every province, and in every city where the king's command and his order came, the Jews had joy and gladness, a feast and a good day. And many of the people of the land became Jews, for the fear of the Jews fell on them.

We begin this account with a really bad decision made by the king. He elevates Haman to the position of viceroy, second in command to the king. Then the king actually instructs that the people bow down to Haman. The bystanders at the gate wonder why Mordecai does not bow down as the rest of them do. So when they see the repeated behavior of Mordecai, they make Haman aware of it. The king's commands were to be obeyed, and if they were disobeyed, it could mean imprisonment or death. It was the king's command that the people bow down to Haman. Mordecai's refusing to do so angered Haman, and he wanted him dead; however, he was aware of Mordecai's position and thought twice about personally attacking him. Mordecai was a member of the king's court, and the seats at the gate were positions of authority. This may be why Haman sought to kill all the Jews, as an edict to kill all Jews would naturally include Mordecai. He did not know that it would also include the queen.

According to the Talmud, the central text of Rabbinic Judaism and the primary source of Jewish law, the presentation of Haman to the king was much more than a simple accusation that the Jews did not obey the law of the king. According to the Talmud, Haman states to the king that there was a people scattered abroad and dispersed among the peoples in all the provinces of his realm. Their laws are different from all the other nations, and they do not observe the king's laws. Therefore, it is not befitting the king to tolerate them. If it pleases the king, let it be recorded that they be destroyed, and I will pay ten thousand silver talents for deposit into the king's treasures. Haman's argument is straightforward and clear: Jews are different. They are alien, outsiders, an obstruction to normal society. They don't fit into the rest of the human family. They have their own faith and their own laws, which they feel are superior to the king's laws. They are a nuisance, a threat, and they ought to be disposed of. The oral tradition of the Talmud describes Haman's presentation even further. They don't eat from our food, they do not marry our women, and they do not marry their women to us. Ironically, at this point in time, they were not aware that the King's wife was a Jew. They waste the whole year avoiding the king's work with the excuse that today is the Sabbath or today is Passover. Haman further argues that the Jews see themselves as superior to us. Choices!

Ironically, another choice was made by both Queen Vashti and the king. The king was having a party for all his princes, and Vashti was having a party for all the women. After many days and after much wine, the king called for Vashti to come before him. He wanted her to come before the princes so that he could show off her beauty. She refused, which was not a good choice. Her refusal might be better understood if taken by the Jewish tradition that she was ordered to appear naked. He asked his wise men what should be done to her, and they said that if she is not punished, all the wives in the land will dishonor their husbands and disobey them. Her refusal either got her banished or possibly killed. Whatever the case, she was no longer the queen. Then the wise men said to have all the young maidens come to the palace and be prepared to come before the king so that he could choose a new queen. Ester was a beauty and she was favored by the one who was overseeing their preparation. Here the king made a really good choice and chose Esther to be his queen. Had he not chosen to have Vashti come before him, and had she not refused, Esther would not have been queen and in a position to save the Jewish people. Choices!

Prior to Haman's approach to the king, the lot was cast, which was called *pur*. Through this process, the date was set. The Hebrew word relating to the casting of lots is *Kashaph* and seems to mean mutter, although the Septuagint (a Greek version of the Hebrew Bible) defines it as being poison. It is also identified as the practice of witchcraft or sorcery. How the casting of the lots actually determined the execution date, we do not know. Whatever the case, the lot was cast at the first of the year, and the execution date was set at the end of the year. The edict was given in the third month, so there was almost nine months from the time of the edict and when it was to be carried out. Choices!

When Mordecai heard of the decree, he began a fasting and mourning period, and so it was throughout the land as the edict was given. Queen Esther found out and was also grieved. She sent clothing to Mordecai to replace his sackcloth, and he refused. So she sent her servant to see exactly what the decree was. Mordecai told the servant all that had happened and sent a copy of the edict to Queen Esther. He also said that she should go before the king on behalf of her people. At first, she refuses. The law concerning approaching the king was very strict. If you were not summoned and entered, and he did not hold out the golden scepter, you would be executed. She sent back a message stating that she had not been summoned to the king for some thirty days. Mordecai sent back a message to Esther and said she should not think that because she was the queen, the edict would not apply to her. If she did not do this then another means of deliverance would be sent by God. I think the next statement is the greatest message of this book, and it shows the hand of God in the deliverance of His people. Who knows whether you have come to the kingdom for such a time as this? Mordecai had faith that God would deliver His people in another way if Esther did not go in to the king, but he also realized that it may well have been the hand of God that placed her in the position she was in. In the following scripture, we have Esther's final answer. Another very important choice.

Esther 4:16 Go, gather all the Jews who are present in Shushan, and fast for me, and do not eat nor drink three days, night or day. My maidservants and I will also fast in the same way. And so I will go in to the king, which *is* not according to the law. And if I perish, I perish. **17** And Mordecai passed over and did according to all that Esther had commanded him.

The favor of God was with her as she approached the king. The time of fasting and prayer had opened the door, and the golden scepter was extended to her. It is amazing that not only was she accepted, but the king offered to grant whatever her request was. Her request would be honored, even if she was to ask for half of the kingdom. She then set the stage for the deliverance of her people. She invites the king and Haman to a banquet she has prepared for them. The king and Haman attend her banquet, and the king inquires as to her request and reiterates the promise of fulfilling it, even to half of the kingdom. She asks that the king and Haman come back the next day for another banquet, and at that time she will reveal her request. Haman goes away joyful and sees Mordecai, who does not move for him nor bow down, and he is immediately filled with anger. He goes home and brags of his wealth and position to his family, and then we see the statement that will be his doom. *Yet all of this avails me nothing as long as I see Mordecai sitting at the king's gate.* Hatred had stolen all joy and satisfaction, even over all of his achievements. His wife and friends reply, have a gallows erected some 50 cubits (70 feet) high and request that the king have Mordecai hanged on the gallows, then go on your merry way to the queen's banquet. Very bad choice!

The favor of God is once again manifested. The king could not sleep that night, which led to another important choice. He commanded that the book of records be brought to him. In the records, he finds that Mordecai had intervened to prevent harm to the king by two of his keepers of the door. The king then asks, what honor or dignity has been done to Mordecai for this? Their reply was that there was nothing done for him. So the king asked who was in the court, and Haman had just entered to entreat the king to hang Mordecai. They told the king that Haman was standing in the court, and the king said show him in. The king asks what should be done for a man the king wants to honor? Haman, thinking that the king wanted to honor him, gave the advice that would humiliate him even further and clearly give a warning against harming Mordecai. So Haman blindly made a choice that would eventually put the noose around his own neck. His hatred of Mordecai would lead to his own death. Can you imagine what it must have been like for him to dress Mordecai in fine apparel and put him on horseback, leading him through the streets proclaiming that this is what the king will do to the one the king desires to honor? Imagine his fear and humiliation!

Now he is going to the queen's banquet and doesn't have a clue that she is a Jew and that his edict would have resulted in her death. Mordecai returns to the king's gate, but Haman hurried home, mourning and having his head covered. Now, his counsel from his family and friends is different. Haman has planned to annihilate the Jews, and Mordecai is a Jew. His family and friends tell him that he will surely not be able to prevail against him and will instead fall before him. His bad choices are about to pay a deadly reward.

Haman and the king attend the second banquet with the queen. Once again, the king asks "what is your request?" She asks that her life be spared and the lives of her people. Informing him that they were sold to be destroyed, to be slain, and to perish. Then the king asks who is he and where is he, that would presume to do such a thing? Then Esther answers and says an adversary and enemy, even this wicked Haman. The king goes into the garden and Haman presumes that he can request his life from the queen after threatening to kill her and her people. He could order the murder of thousands of people and then beg for his own life to be spared. Really! The king returns and finds Haman laying on the queen's couch. Can it get any worse? Would you even force the queen in my own house? As the word went out, they covered Haman's head, and one of the chamberlains pointed out that Haman had built gallows for Mordecai, and the king said let him be hanged on them. What a turn of events from the rejoicing Haman who built the gallows without a clue that they would actually be for him.

Next, the king gives Haman's house to Queen Esther, and the queen informs the king who Mordecai is to her. The king then gave Mordecai the ring that he took from Haman, and Queen Esther put Haman in charge of the house of Haman. Because the king's edict could not be changed or reversed, the king informed Mordecai and Esther to write what they wanted, seal it with the ring, and send the news out to all the provinces. The following portion is the new edict from the king.

Esther 8:11 In *them* the king granted the Jews in every city to gather themselves, and to stand for their life, to destroy, to kill and to cause to perish, all the power of the people and province who desired to attack them, little ones and women, and *to take* what they owned for a prize.

The Jews rejoiced when they saw that they could defend themselves and kill any who tried to kill them. There was also a revival of sorts as many of the people became Jews because they feared for their lives at the hands of the Jews. The Jews killed their enemies, and at the request of Esther, the ten sons of Haman were also hanged on the gallows that their father had built for Mordecai. From this time of deliverance, there was a holiday proclaimed on the day of their deliverance, and it was called Purim, which was in memory of their deliverance from the casting of the lots by Haman.

The events of the Book of Esther were determined by choices. God worked things out for the good of the Jews and exposed wicked Haman, reversing his deadly edict. I would say that Haman got ripped off. Some may say he deserved it and that it was his own fault, as his anger led him to hatred and from there to murder, and in the end, his plot backlashes on him. The sad part of this is that thousands of innocent Jews would have been killed by the choice of one man who was angry with one Jew. Not every negative choice has an immediate or expected or possible outcome. A drunk driver choosing to drive while drunk does not necessarily get pulled over by the police or, God forbid, kill someone. I can't even say that good choices will bring an immediate positive outcome. The point is not to try and predict the outcome of choices but to recognize that it is better to make good choices than to hope for the best out of bad choices. Choices do really matter.

Giving us volition was a choice God made, and it has produced some amazing outcomes. I personally misused that privilege and made some really bad choices. Like Haman, I did not have a clue that the price of my choices would affect my life so drastically. Sadly, my choices also affected others, and the most devastating was that my bad choices also affected some of the people I dearly loved. My choice to accept the salvation offered has directed and changed so many choices over the past fifty years that I could write a book about them, which is what I intend to do. The accumulated effect of my one choice has been amazing. When I realized that God, through the leading of the Holy Spirit, could direct me and that the choices I made could be determined by the awesome counsel of almighty God, I began to go to Him more and more for His direction. Dear reader, I pray that if you have not chosen to accept the loving, sacrificial gift of salvation, that you will make the most important choice of your life and accept Jesus into your heart and follow His counsel.

I would like to close this chapter with a personal testimony of a choice that greatly affected my life and one that I am so thankful for. Shortly after being saved, I was reading a book by David Wilkerson called *The Cross And The Switchblade*. David had shared how, before his ministry opened up to the gangs in New York, the Lord had directed him to spend two hours each morning in prayer and fellowship with Him. I felt like the Lord was speaking this to me as well. At first, I didn't know if I was just being naive and hoping for a ministry as a product of this direction or if God was really directing me to do the same. Finally, in response to what I believed the Lord was telling me to do, I said the following. "Lord, you know that I have ADD and that I cannot sit still for twenty minutes, let alone two hours. The draw toward this commitment was strong and persistent. I finally relented and said if that is what You want, then I will do it, and if I sit there and twiddle my thumbs for two hours, I will still do it. After about twenty minutes of twiddling my thumbs, a miracle happened. I began to hear the Lord more clearly than I had ever heard Him before, and I was not at all anxious. From that time, my growth escalated, and I grew. I still meet with the Lord first every morning.

Chapter 11: The Father's Heart

To misunderstand the heart of God concerning His will and purpose for creating mankind will distort our view of God. If your premise is wrong, all your conclusions will be affected. For instance, if I believe that one plus one equals four, then it would be safe to say that all my mathematical conclusions will be affected because my perception of this basic principle is wrong. My entire understanding of mathematics would be founded on a false premise. So also a false premise of God's heart and purpose for our lives will result in a misunderstanding of His plans and purposes for us. If we do not understand His heart, then we will also misunderstand the purpose of His laws and the resulting penalty of death placed on sin.

Over the years, as a pastor, many Christian couples have come to me for counseling because their marriage was failing. I would ask them, "Why they don't just get a divorce?" and they would look at me in shock and say, "We can't get a divorce." When I ask why, their reply is, "God hates divorce." My next question is, do you think that God is pleased with the relationship you have now, and is it what He intended for your marriage? When they respond in the negative, it leads me to the next question. Why does God hate divorce? We're not sure; we just know that the Word says he hates divorce. I then ask, "Do you think that God has some law concerning divorce written on the walls of heaven, and He is angry with you because you broke His law?" God hates divorce because of what it does to you, your children, parents, brothers and sisters, and friends. It is His heart of love for you that causes the hatred of that which brings destruction to you. Their misunderstanding of God's heart put them at odds with God because they knew they were breaking His law, but they did not understand the heart behind the law. Their view of God was somewhat distorted.

All throughout scripture, God is referred to as Father. From the Lord's Prayer, where the disciples were instructed to pray, our

Father who art in Heaven, to Jesus' repeated declaration that He was sent by His Father. Even from before the beginning of time, God has been identified as the Father of Jesus, His only begotten Son. The book of Hebrews proclaims that it was the Father's desire to bring many sons to glory. Jesus is proclaimed to be the firstborn among many brethren, and the Holy Spirit bears witness that we are the children of God. In the book of Galatians, we find the term *Abba Father* when speaking of our adoption as sons. The term *Abba* is a very personal and intimate term and portrays the trust of a child, apart from reason. *Abba Father* can also be interpreted as my very own Father. If we do not comprehend that God is a loving Father, then we do not see God as He is. This results in a misconception of God and His purposes.

If we do not see God as a loving Father who desires to have an intimate relationship with us, then we will misunderstand Him. There are many biblical examples of God the Father having a relationship with mankind. Adam and Eve were not created so that God could merely observe them in the garden. He walked and fellow shipped with them in the cool of the evening. Abraham, the father of our faith, was called the friend of God. Enoch walked with God and was taken into Heaven without ever facing death. The prophet Elijah, who was the voice of God to His people, also did not face death because God took him to Heaven in a fiery chariot. Moses spoke personally with God on Mount Sinai, and Joshua, his successor, walked with God throughout the conquering of the Promised Land. King David was identified as a man after God's own heart, and the prophets who communed with God were His voice to the people of Israel. Finally, Jesus was the man who had a perfect relationship with the Father, and He prayed that as He and the Father were one that we might be one with them. Although leaders, kings, and prophets had a relationship with the Father, the prophets longed for the future relationship they could see we would have through the sacrifice of Jesus Christ. The price God was willing to pay to remove our sins and thereby open the door for us to have fellowship with Him declares His heart for relationship. If we are born again, then we are born of God and are His children.

Children are one of God's greatest gifts. His heart as a Father and His desire for many children can also be seen through His creation. He designed within the physical makeup of the man and the woman the amazing ability to create life. The love of a child is one of the strongest human loves we will ever experience and gives us a glimpse of God's heart as a parent. Therefore, through our children, we can, to some degree, comprehend the amazing love He has for us. As parents, we most likely would be willing to give our lives for our children; however, few, if any, would ever give the life of their child for another human being. I cannot fully comprehend the love of Jesus, to give His life for us when we were still His enemies, but the Father did more than that. If I correctly understand the heart of the Father, it would have been easier for Him to have come and died than to send His Son to die. One day, when my son Tony was about twelve years old, he told me that he loved me, and I responded with, "I love you too, bud." He then declared that he loved me more than I loved him. I said, "Son, I know you love me, and I realize that you think you love me more, but the love of a son for a father is different than the love of a father for a son." I said one day, he would find a mate and experience a new kind of love for his mate; however, when he had his first child, he would understand what I was talking about. When he called me to give me the good news of the safe delivery of his son Jacob, He said, "Oh, Dad, now I know what you were talking about. Do you really love me that much?" I said, "I always have, and I always will!" Although we can better understand His love for us through our love for our children, His ability to love far supersedes ours.

Our view of our parents' love for us will greatly influence our view of God's love for us. God desires for parents to raise their children with a scriptural view of Him and to demonstrate His love and His desire for fellowship with them. One of the major causes of a distorted view of God comes from a dysfunctional relationship with our parents. The sad truth is, not all children are loved and properly cared for, even by Christian parents. Many children experience a horrible relationship with their parents, and some are victims of abuse. Others have little or no relationship with their parents, while others don't know who their parents are. Although both parents influence their children, I have found over the years that the greatest influence on a child's view of God is their relationship with their father. Since God is our spiritual Father the view we have of our natural father will greatly affect the way we view God. My dad was a good man, and I cannot begin to judge the reasons why he would not spend time with me, but I do know the negative effects it had on me. His lack of praise or encouragement caused me to diligently try to win his approval. His strict discipline when some task was undone, or my behavior was not what he required caused me to greatly fear him. When I was convinced that his approval would never be given, I made every effort to lessen the punishment by doing the best I could to obey his commands or avoid getting caught. As an adult, I could intellectually come up with other reasons for his behavior than it being my fault; however, this did not heal my damaged emotions. Although I could reason that God was not exactly like my dad, I did not know what behavior was like God and what was not. As a result, my view of God was not clear, and in time, I would find out just how distorted it was.

Obviously, the upbringing in the home will affect the life of the child in a negative or positive way. From non-Christian homes, although good people and good parents, the effects of no training and understanding of God and His love for them will have an influence on them, affecting their view of God. Atheist parents will have a very negative effect on their children concerning God the Father. Abusive parents and those trapped in alcoholism and drugs will have a very critical effect on the children as well. Sexual abuse of a father, either on his sons or daughters, will have a seriously damaging effect on seeing God as a father. The point is that the upbringing of a child can greatly influence their view of God.

One of the major ingredients of any good relationship is communication. Readers unfamiliar with scripture may not realize that we are to have a two-way communication with God. I say two ways because many people pray to God but do not realize that they can actually hear from Him. He may not speak in an audible voice, although that is possible; however, He does communicate with His people. There is an inner voice that confirms the Word, and gives us direction for our daily life. Not all things we need direction for are spelled out in the Word. Many personal decisions and directions require what the Bible calls a Rhema word, which stands for a living word or a word made alive to the believer. This is true for every believer, and hearing God is a process that is learned. The scripture declares, *"My sheep hear my voice, and I know them, and they follow me."* I will never forget my first experience of hearing God speak to me. I was working in the coffeehouse ministry one evening, sitting off in a corner by myself, praying. I mentioned to the Lord that I understood that we were to hear His voice, but I was not sure how to do that. I made a commitment that if He would teach me to hear His voice, I would do what He said to do and say what He told me to say. Shortly after this prayer, I noticed a young girl sitting alone, and the thought came to me that I should go over and tell her that God loved her. I reasoned to myself that this was just my mind, and she probably already knew that God loved her. My next thought was, well, I did say that I would obey, and if this is the Lord speaking to me, I want to be obedient. I also realized that telling her that God loves her couldn't do any harm; after all, His Word declares that He does. I determined that I would tell her, so I approached the table and casually said, "I felt impressed from God to come and tell you that He really loves you." She began to weep, and I was not sure what to do next. When she composed herself, she shared with me that before I came over to her, she was praying and asking God if He really loved her. I was thrilled! The possibilities of hearing and obeying God flooded my mind and overwhelmed me. I was actually an answer to her prayer, and there was no way I could have known what her request was if God had not told me. He had allowed me to be His messenger! From that day on, I have been on a quest to talk with God but also to learn to hear His voice and obey.

My response to the Father's call for a personal relationship was not easy. After I got saved, I learned from the scriptures that God wanted to have a Father and son relationship with me. I could not imagine how this could be true, but still, the scriptures said it was. I discovered that I was responding to God's call through my low self-esteem and feelings of inferiority, which I rightly or wrongly attributed to my dad. I was hopelessly trying to discover what God could possibly see in me that merited a relationship with Him. I couldn't imagine why anyone would want a relationship with me, let alone God. When I first came to the Lord, I was simply keeping my end of a bargain and had never even thought about a relationship. It wasn't about His valuing me or wanting to be with me; it was about keeping my Word. This relationship thing was okay with me, but it was more than I had bargained for. I still didn't understand just what He wanted with me, but I did commit to giving Him my life, and if He wanted to spend time with me, that was His business. I decided I would obey and confided in Him that I did not have a clue what this relationship was supposed to look like or how I was to behave. What do I do? I don't know what to expect. Do I just sit here, or do I read the scriptures? I really didn't have a clue. He assured me that if I would give Him the time, He would teach me and that He would take the lead in building the relationship. The understanding of how much time He wanted came to me in a strange way. As I mentioned before, I had just read David Wilkerson's book, *"The Cross And The Switchblade,"* and in it,

David mentions that his life changed drastically when he began to get up early and spend two hours with God each day. I first thought, what in the world would I do for two hours? I had trouble sitting still for ten minutes! I said, God you know that I have ADD and that it is almost impossible for me to sit still, especially for two hours! I knew in my heart that this was what He wanted me to do, so I determined to do just that. I told the Lord that I would give Him the two hours each morning, and if I just sat there twiddling my thumbs for the entire two hours, I would still be there. I remember the first day vividly. I thought for sure after about a half hour that I was going to be tested on my thumb-twiddling commitment. As I sat there, a scripture came to mind, and as I read and meditated on it, I discovered that He was speaking to me as the scripture was relevant to what was going on in my life at the time. At times, I would feel impressed with doing certain things for my wife, and when I followed through, she would give me this questioning look. When I discovered that she had prayed and asked God for the very thing I did, I understood the puzzled look. This really began to increase my faith, and it didn't do so bad for my wife's either. One thing she knew for sure was that I was definitely listening to God. The director of the ministry would tell me that he would be ready to address something in my life, and before he could, it was corrected. I found myself excited to get up in the morning. This Father-son thing was pretty cool!

Romans 12:2 says that we are to be transformed by the *renewing of our mind.* As the relationship continued, I realized that I was still seeing God through the eyes of my damaged emotions and wrong thinking. I became aware that I did have a relationship with my dad, but it just wasn't a good one. We never did spend time together, but we did have a relationship. Our relationship was based on work and discipline. I was assigned tasks, and if they were not done, I was in trouble, but if they were finished properly, there would be no response. I found that I was viewing God's directions as tasks, and if they were not completed properly, I had a difficult time wanting to be with Him. My bad behavior greatly affected my security with God. I would still meet with Him in the morning even though I expected to be rebuked. I was amazed that I did not receive any punishment, and He was never harsh with me. I can't say that I thought my behavior didn't matter to Him, but He wasn't angry and didn't reject me. One morning, He taught me a simple but profound lesson. The lesson was the one I shared earlier in the chapter concerning our distorted viewpoint of God. I had a wrong premise. The obvious question was, how do I change my premise? The answer was to base my view on His Word and to correct my wrong thinking with the scriptures. This was not just a mental process but was directed and affirmed through relationship. One of the major changes came through a revelation of the following scripture. Romans 8:32 says, *He that spared not his own Son, but delivered him up for us all, how shall he not with Him also freely give us all things?* I had read this passage before, but that day, it just broke my heart. I was suddenly and painfully aware of the way I had been treating the Father. What was I thinking? I truly believed that God had sent His Son to die for me, but what I did not see in this sacrifice was the Father's amazing demonstration of love for me. How could I ask Him for any other proof? What greater demonstration could He possibly give? He had held back nothing! He had paid the greatest and dearest price! Through my tears, I asked Him to please forgive me for doubting His love. I felt as if I had been spitting in His face. I declared that I would never again question his love. Once again, He had corrected my view without any harshness. My heart was broken, but He did not break it. It was broken because my love for Him was growing, and I never wanted to hurt Him. I felt His love wash over me, and I have never been the same since. As I gained my composure, I re-read the passage, and the words "freely give" seemed to jump off the page. I wondered if I had misread something. I asked out loud, freely, without cost, without performance? He replied, *the price paid was costly, but it is free to you.* I said, "Who are you?" I didn't wait for an answer; I just told Him that He was more than I had ever dreamed or imagined. From that day on, I knew that His love and acceptance was not based on my behavior but on His amazing love, demonstrated by the price paid by my wonderful savior.

One of the amazing accounts of a father's love is the parable of the return of the prodigal son. It shows the love of the father and his grace and forgiveness. I will copy the account here and make some comments after.

Luke 15:11 And He said, A certain man had two sons. **12** And the younger of them said to *his* father, Father, give me the portion of goods that is coming *to me*. And he divided *his* living to them. **13** And not many days afterward, the younger son gathered all together and went away into a far country. And there he wasted his property, living dissolutely. **14** And when he had spent all, there arose a mighty famine in that land. And he began to be in want. **15** And he went and joined himself to a citizen of that country. And he sent him into his fields to feed pigs. **16** And he was longing to fill his belly with the husks that the pigs ate, and no one gave to him. **17** And when he came to himself, he said, How many hired servants of my father abound in loaves, and I perish with hunger! **18** I will arise and go to my father, and will say to him, Father, I have sinned against Heaven and before you **19** and am no more worthy to be called your son. Make me like one of your hired servants. **20** And he arose and came to his father. But when he was still a great way off, his father saw him and had compassion, and ran and fell on his neck and kissed him. **21** And the son said to him, Father, I have sinned against Heaven and before you, and am no more worthy to be called your son. **22** But the father said to his servants, Bring the best robe and put *it* on him. And put a ring on his hand and shoes on *his* feet. **23** And bring the fattened calf here and kill *it*. And let us eat and be merry, **24** for this my son was dead and is alive again, he was lost and is found. And they began to be merry. **25** And his elder son was in the field. And as he came and drew near the house, he heard music and dancing. **26** And he called one of the servants and asked what these things meant. **27** And he said to him, Your brother has come, and your father has killed the fattened calf because he has received him safe and sound. **28** And he was angry and would not go in. Therefore his father came out and entreated him. **29** And answering he said to *his* father, Lo, these many years I have served you, neither did I transgress your commandment at any time. And yet you never gave *me* a kid so that I might make merry with my friends. **30** But when this son of yours came, who has devoured your living with harlots, you have killed for him the fattened calf. **31** And he said to him, Son, you are always with me, and all that I have is yours. **32** It was right that we should make merry and be glad, for this brother of yours was dead and is alive again; and was lost, and is found.

This parable portrays the love of God and the grace that is given to those who have gone astray and are dead to him. The son was not dead, but he was dead to his father and lost. Now the heart of the wayward brother was to be a servant and no longer an owner, expecting to be treated as one. He realized he had failed his father and was foolish in doing so. The father's heart was to forgive and celebrate his return. So it is with God the Father who will give forgiveness and grace to all who come to him no matter what the offense or foolishness of the life lived. The contrast is the brother who was upset because he was welcomed back and forgiven all, and that the father was celebrating his return. His complaint also was that he had been faithful and had not left the father and yet had not had a fattened calf given for him and a celebration of the things he had done in staying. The surprising thing is that the son did not know that as far as the father was concerned, he had always been with him and that everything he had was his. May we also not be offended at the forgiveness of God for those we may not believe deserve it. We should welcome any who come into the fold and are saved. The Father forgives and accepts all who will come to him. Those of us who are His children will be freely given all that is needed. If He spared not His own Son, will he not freely give us all things with Him?

God's love and desire for a relationship is the gospel. It is the good news! It is not all that is contained within the will of God for us, but it is the power of God for salvation. To miss a personal, intimate relationship with the Father is to miss the very heart of God.

Dear reader, my prayer for you is that you would know the love of the Father and His perfect will and purpose for your life. Some of you may already know that, and I praise God for it. If you do not know the love of the Father and have not accepted the salvation He provided, I pray that you would. You will not be sorry for accepting the sacrifice and love of the Father and His glorious Son, and the Holy Spirit will come and live within you. God has a plan for you, and it is better than any plan you could come up with on your own. May you find the Father's heart, and for those of you who know Him, may you grow in His love and care.

Chapter 12: Blessed Assurance

The security of salvation is an issue that troubles many who are truly born again but still fear they may not make it into Heaven. We are to walk by faith and not by sight and do so from salvation until we enter Heaven. We believe in a God we have never seen, and that is the reality of the walk of faith. We walk by faith and not by sight. God does not leave us alone on this walk but leads and provides for us as we fellowship with Him. Our faith will grow as we continue our walk, and we can grow in our trust in Him and in His faithfulness to His Word. He has promised to never leave us nor forsake us, and we can trust that what He starts, He is more than able to finish. He is the Alpha and Omega, the beginning and the end. We are saved by grace, and we will enter Heaven on the same basis. We can never earn it! Yes, we are to grow, but we are not cast aside when we err. The apostle Paul wrote the following portion of scripture to the Philippians to assure them that God does finish what He starts and that the one who started a good work in them would complete it.

Philippians 1:6 being confident of this very thing, that He who has begun a good work in you will perform *it* until the day of Jesus Christ,

For each of us, the day of Jesus Christ may be when we die and leave this earth to be with Him, or it may be when He returns for the church. The point is that He is faithful to complete what He begins. In the book of John we have the following amazing statement:

John 6:44 No one can come to Me unless the Father who has sent Me draw him, and I will raise him up at the last day.

If you are born again, you had to come to Jesus for salvation, as there is no salvation in any other. If you are born again, then from this scripture it is clear that it did not happen by chance, as it could not have happened unless the Father drew you. The drawing is not a forced drawing as the word is used in some passages to represent one being drawn to the executioner. The word used in this passage means a gracious allurement. There is no doubt that we have a free will and are not forced to accept salvation, but the drawing toward it is from God. You may argue that God probably draws everyone, but that is not the point I am making. The point is, if you are born again, it happened because He drew you, and you made a choice to receive the salvation offered. You were not forced but drawn, and God was involved in the drawing. If I connect the reality that the Father actually drew me and realize that I would never have been saved if He had not, then I can also believe that Jesus will finish what He has started. It is not my working it out and trying to keep my salvation by works, as I could not be saved by works, and I cannot keep my salvation by works. I believe the following portion, also written by the apostle Paul, has caused some concern along this line.

Philippians 2:12 Therefore, my beloved, as you have always obeyed, not as in my presence only, but now much more in my absence, cultivate your own salvation with fear and trembling. **13** For it is God who works in you both to will and to do of *His* good pleasure.

Paul is not speaking of earning our salvation or of holding on to it by works, but working out our walk with God. We are a part of that walk, as we are not robots. We do not lose our ability to choose just because we have accepted Jesus as savior. Earlier in the book, we looked at the reality that when we are saved, it is not the end but a new beginning, and we are to be transformed by the renewing of the mind and what that meant. We are to walk by faith with God, and God does not do it all, and we do not do it all, but we do the work together. We are also in a war. The fear and trembling is not a terror but a reverence for God and an awareness that the enemy is to be dealt with. Sin is never good, and the enemy will not relent in his efforts to distract us from the will of God and to entangle us in fear and disobedience. We do not have to fear the enemy, but understand that he is an enemy and we must be aware of the potential dangers of not staying clear of his lies and temptations. God is on our side, and He will lead us and make us aware of the traps and lies of the enemy. The end of the above scripture says that it is God who works in you both to will and to work for his good pleasure. It is His good pleasure to have you as his child and to walk with you and finish the race set before you. If you are a born-again believer, then you were drawn by God to Jesus, who is the only means of salvation and the author and finisher of our faith. We are secure in Him, and He is more than able to finish what He started.

Hebrews 6 has also been a potion that the enemy has used to threaten us with the fear of losing our salvation. The chapter begins with instructions to continue with the growth that is a part of salvation by leaving the basic doctrines of salvation and moving on to the growth that God wants for us.

Hebrews 6:1 Therefore, having left the discourse of the beginning of Christ, let us go on to full growth, not laying again the foundation of repentance from dead works, and of faith toward God, **2** of *the* baptisms, of doctrine, and of laying on of hands, and of resurrection of the dead, and of eternal judgment. **3** And this we will do, if God permits. **4** For *it is* impossible for those who were once enlightened, and have tasted of the heavenly gift, and were made partakers of *the* Holy Spirit, **5** and have tasted *the* good Word of God and *the* powers of the world to come, **6** and who have fallen away; it is impossible, I say, to renew them again to repentance, since they crucify the Son of God afresh to themselves and put *Him* to an open shame. **7** (For the earth which drinks in the rain that comes often upon it, and brings forth plants fit for those by whom it is dressed, receives blessing from God. **8** But *that which* bears thorns and briers *is* rejected and *is* a curse, whose end *is* to be burned.)

This portion clearly says that if one continues to reject Jesus, even after being born again, salvation can be lost. I know that sounds contradictory to what I have just said, but it is really not. We do not lose the ability to choose, and we could, in fact, choose to have nothing more to do with Jesus and deny Him as our savior. If we did so, then there would remain no more means of salvation since He is the only means of salvation. It would take a complete rejection of Jesus as our savior and Lord and a denial of who He is. He is the means, the only means of salvation; therefore to reject Him as savior would result in loss of salvation. I am not sure what would cause such a decision but I know that it would be the work of the enemy and the acceptance and belief of his lies. Whatever the reason, a complete rejection of Jesus as savior would mean a loss of salvation. This would seem to imply that a continued disobedience leading to a rejection of Christ would mean that He would let you go. It would rule out the discipline of the Lord that He gives to His children whom He loves. There is a major difference between discipline and punishment. Punishment is an act of retribution which says since you did this to me, I will do this to you. Discipline is a loving action taken for the good of the person being disciplined, for the purpose of preventing their harm and potential destruction. If my little child attempted to go out onto the road into traffic, I would obviously teach him not to do so. If he continued, I would discipline him, and if he continued to disobey, I would continue to discipline him, but not for the purpose of having it my way, but for his protection. Sometimes, we are like little children and need to grow up, and God will take action to protect us through His loving discipline. I would put a fence up if I had to until my child would learn of the danger of going into the road. I would hope that one day my child would know the reality of the dangers of walking out in front of an oncoming vehicle and wait until it passed. We need to know the same about the sins and other bad decisions God wants us to avoid. My point is that I would not just say, "Oh well, I warned you, but you wouldn't listen, so you can just pay the price." What God starts, He fully intends to finish, but it doesn't mean that we have lost our ability to choose. Our salvation is not a simple one-time choice, but our choice is to accept Jesus, both as savior and Lord. The lie right from the beginning with Adam and Eve was that God was withholding from them and depriving them of what was really good for them, namely the deadly fruit. How foolish would it be to think there was something good about walking out in front of an oncoming vehicle? God is for us and not against us, and discipline is for our good. I cannot imagine what it would take to cause someone who has once been enlightened and tasted of the heavenly gift, and were made partakers of the Holy Spirit, and tasted the good word of God, and the powers of the age to come, and then fell away. I wonder about the amount of times that God will discipline His child, and will He not make every effort to prevent the loss of salvation once given? He will surely not easily discard His children; it would be the result of their continued rebellion and ultimate rejection of Jesus.

God in the end, through the anointing of the Holy Spirit, directed the author of Hebrews to make it very clear that He is faithful to His Word, and we can be assured of our salvation and our ultimate reward of eternal life in Heaven.

Hebrews 6:13-20: For when God made promise to Abraham, since he could swear by none greater, he swore by himself, 14 saying, Surely blessing I will bless thee, and multiplying I will multiply thee. 15 And thus, having patiently endured, he obtained the promise. 16 For men swear by the greater: and in every dispute of theirs, the oath is final for confirmation. 17 Wherein God, being minded to show more abundantly unto the heirs of the promise the immutability of his counsel, interposed with an oath; 18 that by two immutable things, in which it is impossible for God to lie, we may have a strong encouragement, who have fled for refuge to lay hold of the hope set before us: 19 which we have as an anchor of the soul, a hope both sure and steadfast and entering into that which is within the veil; 20 whither as a forerunner Jesus entered for us, having become a high priest for ever after the order of Melchizedek.

God goes way beyond what, to me, would seem reasonable. His simply saying something should be enough. He cannot lie, and therefore what he says is the truth, and it does not seem necessary for Him to further affirm it. However, God, wanting to show His love and commitment in light of the warning of the previous scriptures, does so by showing abundantly to the heirs of the promise His assurance of the immutability of His counsel. Immutability means that His counsel is unchanging over time, or unable to be changed. He continues with another step in giving an oath to confirm. An oath was a legal context by which one could confirm the truth of one's statement. In so doing, we have two immutable things that cannot be changed, namely God's word and the fact that God cannot lie. These promises are to be an anchor to our soul. We discussed the soul, being the mind, will, and emotions, and this is where the battle is fought, and God's promise to take us through is an anchor to the soul. It is that which holds it steady in one place and does not allow it to be carried away with the lies of the enemy. His attack is on our minds and emotions, and he will use every effort to mislead and damage us through this battle. We can be absolutely sure of our salvation and that Jesus will take us through whatever we face in this life and deliver us to the Father at the close of our time here on earth. God took considerable effort to assure us of His faithfulness and the security of our salvation.

We have another amazing promise and assurance of God's faithfulness and our ultimate victory. We are sealed by the Holy Spirit. In Ephesians 1:13, we have the promise of the seal of the Holy Spirit. The seal is not a what, but a who, and it is the Holy Spirit that is given to the believer as a seal of their redemption. To be sealed with the Holy Spirit is God's gracious gift. It is a seal of His authority and ownership of us as His children and commitment to his people. The Holy Spirit also provides the inner assurance that we are His children. We also have the gift of the Holy Spirit as a guarantee of our inheritance. He will empower us to overcome all obstacles and live a holy life. He will also fight for us, as well as intercede for us. He will certainly protect us through any trials and temptations. What an amazing gift!

I would like to end this final chapter with a portion that is my favorite portion of scripture and has to do with assurance of His call and the finishing of the work He begins. I won't use the entire chapter, but I will detail the portion that speaks to the subject of this chapter. I will copy the portion here and then expound on each verse. It is important to remember that although this was penned by the apostle Paul, it was not His own opinions but was given by the inspiration and direction of the Holy Spirit.

Romans 8:28 And we know that all things work together for good to those who love God, to those who are called according to *His* purpose. **29** For whom He foreknew, He also predestined *to be* conformed to the image of His Son, for Him to be *the* Firstborn among many brothers. **30** But whom He predestined, these He also called; and whom He called, those He also justified. And whom He justified, these He also glorified. 31 What then shall we say to these things? If God *is* for us, who *can be* against us? **32** Truly *He* who did not spare His own Son, but delivered Him up for us all, how shall He not with Him also freely give us all things? **33** Who shall lay anything to the charge of God's elect? *It is* God who justifies. **34** Who *is* he condemning? *It is* Christ who has died, but rather also *who is* raised, who is also at *the* right *hand* of God, who also intercedes for us. **35** Who shall separate us from the love of Christ? *Shall* tribulation, or distress, or persecution, or famine, or nakedness, or peril, or sword? **36** As it is written, "For Your sake we are killed all the day long. We are counted as sheep of slaughter." **37** But in all these things we more than conquer through Him who loved us. **38** For I am persuaded that neither death, nor life, nor angels, nor principalities, nor powers, nor things present, nor things to come, **39** nor height, nor depth, nor any other creature, shall be able to separate us from the love of God which is in Christ Jesus our Lord.

What a broad scope that this first verse addresses — All things! That is the difficult things in life, the failure in our lives, and even the attacks of the enemy. This is a promise to those that love God and those called according to His purpose. The scriptures also tell us that if we love God, we will keep His commandments. I used to look at keeping His commandments as the means of proving that I loved God and thereby receiving the promise of this scripture. However, it is not a matter of proving our love, but a love response of obedience in keeping His commandments. Obedience is a reciprocation of His love for us. We are motivated by love to walk with the Lord in obedience to His guidance and commandments. We grow in love as we grow in faith from our experience of His love and faithfulness. We experience and know His love through our walk with Him in a personal relationship. The scripture also says that we love God because He first loved us. His love reached out to us through the sacrifice of His son and freed us from sin, and made us children of the King. The last part of this verse states that we are called according to His purpose. Being called according to His purpose is true for each of His children, although His purpose for each may vary. There are purposes that apply to all, but there are specific purposes that apply to each. His calling was according to His purpose, and not just for our individual benefit and blessing in living our own lives as we see fit. The promise of all things working together for good is for every person who is called by God. It may be difficult to see how some things that happen in our lives could possibly be for good, but in the end, it is the promise of God that He will work them out for our good.

The next verse is not a matter of predestination, as though God made the choice, and we have nothing to do with it. The predetermined path for each of us was determined on the basis of foreknowledge. God knew you from before the beginning of creation. God is not bound by time but is eternal. He created time and is able to view time from the beginning to the end. Because He knew who would be His does not mean that He determined who was His. If I were to put this in a family setting and act as God in determining who

160

would be saved and who would not, then it would be more clear as to what this would actually mean. As a father, if I said one son could be saved but the other would go to hell, the one son and the one daughter will be saved, but the other children will go to hell. God does not want anyone to perish or go to hell. He would love for every person who has ever existed to be in Heaven with Him. Our salvation is not a matter of His choice but ours. It was a gift of God to give us choice (volition) and to be like Him in that we are able to choose. We do have free will, but free will is not a free pass to reject Christ and live as we want to live. As I have said before, salvation is not a "get out of jail free" card. To assume that we would know better which path and purpose for our lives is obviously a deception. The corporate purpose for our lives is to be conformed to the image of Jesus, that Jesus might be the Firstborn among many brethren. My personal calling as a pastor was a specific calling and a preordained path according to the foreknowledge of God. My calling obviously does not apply to everyone, although we are all truly ministers.

The next verse continues the theme. Again, whom He did predestine on the basis of foreknowledge, He called. Whom He called them He justified, and whom He justified them he also glorified. I think it is important to observe that the pronoun used in this verse is He, and not me or we. He is the one who started our lives with Him, and He is the One who will complete it. According to His foreknowledge, He called us. When I got saved, I did not know that He was calling me, but I knew that I needed to be saved. Again, the call is based on the foreknowledge that we would accept the call. The offer of salvation is to all and not restricted by God in any way. Because He knew beforehand who would accept the salvation offered was not based on His determination of who would be saved, but was a directive for His call. Those whom He called He justified. I have heard justification described as just as if I had never sinned. As far as God is concerned, this is true. He remembers our sins no more. Finally, those whom he justified He glorified. I believe to be glorified is to be conformed to the image of His son. What could be more glorious than to be like Jesus. If you are a born-again believer, God called you, and He will finish the work He started in you.

Romans 31: *What shall we then say to these things? If God be for us, who can be against us?* It is not a matter of if, but it would be more accurately said, since God is for us. Who could possibly defeat or overpower God. Certainly, the enemy is against us, but He cannot win against us as God is for us. The enemy is never for us, and God is never against us! God knew before He called us every mistake and sin we had committed and every sin we would commit after being saved. He knew we would need to grow through the process of conforming to the image of His dear son. He also knew that there would be failures and actual intended sins. He also knows the end of the story, and He is more than able to take us through. We are saved by grace, which is God's unmerited favor, but grace is also God's power by which we can actually be conformed to the image of Jesus. Jesus never sinned and was therefore a perfect sacrifice for those of us who have sinned and still do sin. Sin is never a good thing, and by His grace, we can overcome any and all sin. Jesus broke the power of sin, and we are not condemned to continue to sin. We need not continue to ask for forgiveness for sins over and over again; we need to ask and accept deliverance from all sin. The penalty of death is on sin, and Jesus came that we might have life and have it abundantly. Don't believe the lie that you want to sin, as it is no longer a part of who you are. You no longer have a fallen nature separated from God, but you are a new creation, and therefore it is not in your nature to sin. It is actually against your nature to sin. The flesh can indeed be tempted to sin, but we are not flesh and blood but a born-again spiritual being, and we do not have to abide by the evil desires of the flesh.

Romans 8:32 He that spared not his own Son, but delivered him up for us all, how shall he not with him also freely give us all things?

This is an amazing promise. If we consider the fact that God gave His only begotten son for us, and in fact delivered Him up for us all, the question that demands an answer is: why would He not also with Him give us all things. Could anything God could give us compare with what was given. The Bible says that perhaps for a good man someone might give his life. I might, by the grace of God, give my life for someone, but I would not give the life of my son for anyone. Jesus also gave His life for us out of love for the Father and love for us. How could we believe that God is withholding from us when He did not withhold His only Son. What greater statement could He make for the fact that He is for us and not against us and not withholding any good thing from us. I can also trust my heavenly Father to withhold anything that is not good for me. At times, He may withhold what would damage or even destroy us, while others may be able to handle it. All of my sons wanted to drive, but when they were young boys, they were not allowed to do so. It would have destroyed their lives as well as others. It is not a matter of what I can get from God but that He knows best and has the best in mind for me. What better proof could He possibly give that He has not already proven in the gift of His glorious son? How could I not love and trust someone who cares that much for me? I know that it is for all who would come, but it is also personal. Our love and obedience is also personal to Him.

Romans 8:33 Who shall lay anything to the charge of God's elect? *It is* God who justifies. **34** Who *is* he condemning? *It is* Christ who has died, but rather also *who is* raised, who is also at *the* right *hand* of God, who also intercedes for us.

This is our biggest battle against the condemnation of the enemy. He has no right to lay any charge against us, and it is God who justifies us. Furthermore, Jesus is praying for us according to the will of the Father. We can trust that His prayers, as well as the prayers of the Holy Spirit, who also intercedes for us, will be heard and answered. If our heart is for His will to be done, then we can know and agree with the prayers of Jesus and the Holy Spirit.

Romans 8:35 Who shall separate us from the love of Christ? *Shall* tribulation, or distress, or persecution, or famine, or nakedness, or peril, or sword? **36** As it is written, "For Your sake we are killed all the day long. We are counted as sheep of slaughter." **37** But in all these things we more than conquer through Him who loved us. **38** For I am persuaded that neither death, nor life, nor angels, nor principalities, nor powers, nor things present, nor things to come, **39** nor height, nor depth, nor any other creature, shall be able to separate us from the love of God which is in Christ Jesus our Lord.

What a promise for those who are born-again believers. No matter what we may face on this earth, it can never separate us from the love of God. Literally, since God is for us and not against us, who then can ever separate us from Him and His love for us? We are by His grace more than conquerors, and He will protect us and take us through whatever we may face on this earth. Nothing or no one can ever separate us from the love of God in Christ Jesus our Lord. How could we be more secure in our salvation than that?

The reality is that I am no more saved now than I was the day I got saved, and I am saved for all eternity. I am a different person because, at salvation, I became a new creation. My behavior is different as I have grown and changed from the lifestyle of the old man. The short span of this life in comparison with eternity is nothing, even if I live to be a hundred years old. Why should I ever be concerned about when I go to Heaven or how many years I have on this earth? The truth is I am going to live forever, just not forever on this earth.

My prayer for you, if you are not born again, is that you would come to Jesus and accept Him as Lord and Savior. You will never regret it. He is awesome! If you are already born again, then my prayer is that you will live by faith and walk in obedience to the Lord. Don't live your life less than what He has for you, and may you be greatly blessed as you follow after Him. I don't know when, but I do know that if you are born again, I will see you on the other side.

About the Author

I grew up in an Assemblies of God church, and my dad was the associate pastor. I was in church four to five times a week, until I turned eighteen and rebelled. The next seven years were very destructive and in 1973 my wife and I were saved at a crusade in Detroit Michigan. I have been in the ministry for the past fifty years, in a number of different positions. I started ministry on the streets as an evangelist, I have been a deacon, elder, senor pastor, and have been a part of a ministry to Israel, traveling there fourteen times. The reality that I went to church for eighteen years of my life, and to the altar many times, weeping and repenting, and yet was never saved is daunting, and the reason I wrote this book.

The book has two main messages. First, that God loves you, and sent His son to die for you, so that He might have a relationship with you. What greater love could be demonstrated than for God to give His only begotten son, for you. Secondly, to expose the lie of the enemy that one can get into heaven through religious practices. The scriptures are clear that you must be born again.

MKJV: John 3:3 Jesus answered and said to him, Truly, truly, I say to you, Unless a man is born again, he cannot see the kingdom of God.

The reality that literally millions of good people who are faithful to attend church regularly, give to the poor and do all manner of religious activities, and yet are not saved is heart breaking. Jesus made it very clear in the following scripture reference.

MKJV Matthew 7:21 Not everyone who says to Me, Lord! Lord! shall enter the kingdom of Heaven, but he who does the will of My Father in Heaven. 22 Many will say to Me in that day, Lord! Lord! Did we not prophesy in Your name, and through Your name throw out demons, and through Your name do many wonderful works? 23 And then I will say to them I never knew you! Depart from Me, those working lawlessness!

There is no judgment or criticism in my heart for anyone, and I hope that I have truly represented that. I pray that those who read this book, those who have not been born again, but have trusted in religious practices for their salvation, would come to the Father and accept His love and invitation to be His child. If you have never accepted Christ I pray that this book would be a welcomed invitation. Hopefully, what I have shared will be an encouragement to all Christians.

www.ingramcontent.com/pod-product-compliance
Lightning Source LLC
LaVergne TN
LVHW052027080426
835513LV00018B/2199